The New Creative Crock-Pot® Slow Cooker Cookbook

THE NEW CREATIVE
CROCK-POT®
SLOW COOKER COOKBOOK

Robin Taylor Swatt

Pascoe Publishing
Rocklin, California

Cover design by Salmon Associates
Page design by Melanie Haage Design

Published in the United States by
Pascoe Publishing
Rocklin, California
http://www.pascoepublishing.com

ISBN: 1-929862-09-1

Library of Congress Control Number: 2001093205

04   05   10   9   8   7

Printed in the United States of America

TABLE OF CONTENTS

	Introduction	9
Chapter 1	Crock-Pot® Slow Cooker Hints & Tips	11
Chapter 2	Savory Sauces, Appetizers & Side Dishes	15
Chapter 3	Hearty Crock-Pot® Slow Cooker Beef, Pork & Lamb Recipes	43
Chapter 4	Tempting Crock-Pot® Slow Cooker Chicken & Turkey Dishes	67
Chapter 5	Flavorful Crock-Pot® Slow Cooker Fish & Shellfish Recipes	89
Chapter 6	Favorite Crock-Pot® Slow Cooker Recipes From Around the World	99
Chapter 7	Fast & Easy Crock-Pot® Slow Cooker Meals for Busy Cooks	125
Chapter 8	Lowfat Crock-Pot® Slow Cooker Meals for Healthy Living	147
Chapter 9	Delectable Crock-Pot® Slow Cooker Dessert Recipes	187
	Index	215

ACKNOWLEDGMENTS

Thank you to my husband, Jeff Swatt, for his love, support and never-ending appetite for Crock-Pot® slow cooker cooking. And, of course, thank you to my Mom, Emiko, for being my culinary inspiration by cooking amazing meals each and every day.

—Robin Taylor Swatt

INTRODUCTION

For over thirty years, Rival's Crock-Pot® slow cooker has changed the way Americans cook for their families. The Crock-Pot® slow cooker is a convenient way to provide a home-cooked meal for families on the go - just plug it in, enjoy your day, and rest assured that when you come home, a delicious, nutritious meal will be waiting for you!

We hope you enjoy this new cookbook. Great care has been taken to ensure that the recipes are unique and inventive, and reflect the tastes of today's slow cooker chefs. Each recipe is designed for our 3 to 4 quart slow cooker, with additional instructions for increasing the recipe ingredients to fit the larger sizes of slow cookers. An easy way to estimate how much food your Crock-Pot® slow cooker will optimally cook is to use a "pounds per quart" comparison. For every pound of meat you cook, estimate 1 quart of cooker space. For example, a 4 pound roast would fit a 4 quart slow cooker and a 3 pound chicken would fit a 3 quart slow cooker.

For some more delicious recipe ideas, or to send a message to our chef, visit us at www.crock-pot.com. We'd love to hear from you! But for now, plug in your slow cooker and start cooking!

Sincerely,

The Rival® Kitchen

CHAPTER 1

CROCK-POT® SLOW COOKER HINTS & TIPS

1. *Stirring*

Due to the nature of slow cooking, there is no need to stir the food unless it specifically says to in your recipe. In fact, taking the lid off to stir food causes the slow cooker to lose a significant amount of heat, extending the cooking time required. Therefore, it is best not to remove the lid for stirring or even just for a "peek."

2. *Adding Ingredients at the End of the Cooking Time*

Certain ingredients should be added toward the end of the cooking time. These include:

- ◆ Milk and sour cream should be added during the last 15 minutes of cooking time.
- ◆ Seafood should be added in the last hour of cooking time, unless the recipe specifies otherwise.

3. *Pasta and Rice*

For best results with pasta, cook in a pot of boiling water until just tender. Add the pasta to the stoneware during the last half hour of cooking.

For best results with rice, always use long grain converted rice. If it doesn't seem to cook completely after the suggested time, you may try adding an extra 1 to 1½ cup of liquid per cup of rice.

4. Beans

It is best to boil beans before cooking them in the Crock-Pot® slow cooker. Cook the beans in water on the stovetop until tender and then add them to the stoneware.

5. Cooking with Frozen Foods

You can cook frozen meats in your Crock-Pot® slow cooker, however it is best to use the following guidelines:

- Add at least 1 cup of warm liquid to the stoneware before placing the meat in the stoneware.
- Do not preheat the unit.
- Cook recipes containing frozen meats for an additional 4 to 6 hours on Low or 2 hours on High.

6. Cooking Temperatures and Food Safety

Cooking meats in your Crock-Pot® slow cooker is perfectly safe. According the U.S. Department of Agriculture, bacteria in food is killed at a temperature of 165°F. Meats cooked in the Crock-Pot® slow cooker reach an internal temperature of 170°F in beef and as high as 190°F in poultry. It is important to follow the recommended cooking times and to the keep the cover on your slow cooker during the cooking process.

7. Removable Stoneware

The Removable Stoneware in your Crock-Pot® slow cooker makes it easy to prepare food ahead of time, and makes cleaning easy. Here on some tips on the use and care of your stoneware:

- When you're ready to cook food that has been refrigerated in the stoneware, place the stoneware on the heating base and turn the temperature control to the desired setting.

The bowl and food do not need to be allowed to come to room temperature before heating. Use the maximum cooking time.

♦ Do not preheat the slow cooker.

♦ Your Crock-Pot® slow cooker makes a great server for hot beverages or dips. Keep it on the Low setting to maintain the proper serving temperature.

8. Browning Meat

Due to the nature of slow cooking, meat does not brown as it would if it were cooked in a skillet or oven. It is not necessary to brown meat before slow cooking, however, if you prefer the flavor and look of browned meat, brown your meat in a skillet with a little oil, then place the meat in the stoneware and follow the recipe as usual.

9. Herbs and Spices

When cooking with your Crock-Pot® slow cooker, it is best to use whole herbs and spices rather than crushed or ground. The flavor of crushed or ground herbs and spices seems to lessen during the extended cooking time with the slow cooker. Fresh herbs and spices take longer to release their flavor, and therefore withstand the extended cooking times required of slow cooking.

10. Cooking Breads and Cakes

Here are some tips on making the delicious cakes found in the Dessert chapter of this book!

♦ Do not over-beat breads and cakes. Follow all recommended mixing times.

♦ Do not add water to the slow cooker unless it specifically says to in the recipe.

- After breads and cakes have finished cooking, allow them to cool for 5 minutes before removing from the cake pan.
- The breads and cakes in this cookbook can be cooked in the stoneware. However, for best results, you should use the Crock-Pot® Bread 'N Cake Pan. You may purchase one by calling 1-800-577-4825 or at www.crock-pot.com.

CHAPTER 2

SAVORY SAUCES, APPETIZERS & SIDE DISHES

Your Crock-Pot® slow cooker is an especially convenient appliance when preparing appetizers for a party. Typically, one tries to create menu starters that are easy to make, delicious, impressive and require little or no clean-up. An impossible task? Your Crock-Pot® slow cooker is the perfect tool to create an ultimate appetizer menu for a party and to make the impossible possible. Imagine your guests arriving to the tantalizing aromas of slow cooker hors d'oeuvres, which you made with little effort. Just hours before (or even the night before), you easily combined the necessary ingredients to create amazing appetizers that are true party favorites. You can choose to serve these delicious starters in your own elegant party platters, or even in the stoneware itself. The food is delicious and clean-up is a breeze. Best of all, these appetizers are so easy to make that you can concentrate your culinary energies on main courses and decadent desserts.

Similarly, the slow cooker is a helpful tool in creating side dishes that complement each meal. Just prepare the ingredients, combine them in the stoneware, cover and cook! Instead of focusing your attention on these accompaniments, you can rest assured that your supplemental, but integral side dishes will cook effortlessly in the slow cooker while you work on other aspects of a fabulous meal.

In addition to appetizers and side dishes, your slow cooker can aid your efforts in orchestrating a beautiful and elegant brunch. A perfect appliance for breakfast casseroles, your slow cooker will turn out savory brunch courses while you attend to other components of your morning meal. While you are picking up croissants at your local bakery or arranging flowers on the table, your slow cooker is doing the work for you, and you will return to your kitchen to find a perfectly-cooked main breakfast course.

Included in this chapter are recipes for appetizers that are tried and true party favorites. Each is exceedingly simple to prepare, tasty and will impress even the most discerning palate. Also included are recipes for quick side dishes that are fresh and flavorful accompaniments to any meal, as well as brunch recipes that will perfectly start your day.

ARTICHOKE CHEESE DIP

1 lb. mozzarella cheese, shredded
1 cup Parmesan cheese, grated
1 cup mayonnaise
1 cup artichoke hearts, drained and chopped
1 red pepper, seeded and finely chopped
2 cloves garlic, minced

This easy dip is always a party favorite. Your guests will congregate around the Crock-Pot® slow cooker to get every last bit. Serve with sliced baguettes or your favorite crackers.

Add all ingredients to the Crock-Pot® slow cooker and mix thoroughly. Cover; cook on High about 1 hour. Makes enough dip for 15 people.

For larger parties, you can double or even triple the recipe, using the 5, 6 or 7-quart Crock-Pot® slow cooker.

GREEN CHILE CORN DIP

This simple appetizer is a perfect prelude to a Southwest-inspired feast. Serve with white or blue corn tortilla chips.

1 lb. Jack cheese, shredded
1 cup Parmesan cheese, shredded
1 cup mayonnaise
½ cup creamed corn
½ cup fresh or frozen corn kernels
1–4 oz. can diced green chilies
2 cloves garlic, minced
1 Tbs. red pepper flakes
1 Tbs. sun-dried tomatoes, reconstituted and finely chopped

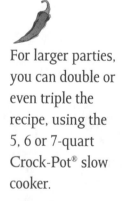

For larger parties, you can double or even triple the recipe, using the 5, 6 or 7-quart Crock-Pot® slow cooker.

Add all ingredients to the Crock-Pot® slow cooker and mix thoroughly. Cover; cook on High about 1 hour. Makes enough dip for 15 people.

CREAMY SPINACH DIP

12 oz. cream cheese, cubed
½ cup heavy whipping cream
10 oz. frozen chopped spinach
1 envelope dry onion soup mix
1 tsp. prepared hot sauce
½ cup green onions, finely sliced
1 tsp. fresh lemon juice

You can present this warm version of classic spinach dip in the Crock-Pot® slow cooker or ladled into a sourdough bread bowl. Serve with raw vegetables, your favorite crackers or sourdough bread pieces.

Combine the cream cheese and whipping cream in the Crock-Pot® slow cooker. Cover and heat on High until the cheese is melted, about 45 minutes. Add the spinach, soup mix and prepared hot sauce, and stir thoroughly. Cover; cook on High for 30 minutes. Shortly before serving, add the green onions and lemon juice and mix thoroughly again.

For larger parties, you can double or even triple the recipe, using the 5, 6 or 7-quart Crock-Pot® slow cooker.

HOT CRAB DIP

This beloved crab appetizer is a popular request for many a party. Serve with potato chips or water crackers.

12 oz. cream cheese, cubed
¼ cup heavy whipping cream
1 cup Parmesan cheese
2–6½ oz. cans lump crab meat
1 envelope dry onion soup mix
1 Tbs. Worcestershire sauce
2 cloves garlic, minced
1 tsp. fresh lemon juice
salt to taste
fresh chives, minced, for garnish

For larger parties, you can double or even triple the recipe, using the 5, 6 or 7-quart Crock-Pot® slow cooker.

Combine the cream cheese and whipping cream in the Crock-Pot® slow cooker. Cover and heat on High until the cheese is melted, about 45 minutes. Add the Parmesan cheese, crab meat, onion soup mix, Worcestershire sauce, and garlic and stir thoroughly. Cover; cook on High for 30 minutes. Shortly before serving, add the lemon juice and mix thoroughly. Salt to taste. Sprinkle the top with fresh minced chives as a garnish.

ASIAN SPICED CHICKEN WINGS

3 lbs. chicken wings
1 cup soy sauce
1 cup brown sugar
½ cup ketchup
2 tsp. fresh ginger, minced
2 cloves garlic, minced
¼ cup dry sherry
½ cup hoisin sauce
1 Tbs. fresh lime juice
3 Tbs. sesame seeds, toasted
¼ cup green onions, thinly sliced

Chicken wings are always crowd pleasers. Garnishing them with toasted sesame seeds and green onions gives these appetizers added crunch and contrasting color.

Broil the chicken wings 10 minutes on each side, or until browned. Transfer the chicken wings to the Crock-Pot® slow cooker. Add the remaining ingredients, except the hoisin sauce, lime juice, sesame seeds, and green onions and stir thoroughly. Cover; cook on Low 5 to 6 hours (or on High for 2 to 3 hours). Stir once in the middle of cooking to baste the wings with sauce. Remove the wings from the stoneware and reserve ¼ cup of the juice in the slow cooker. Combine this juice with the hoisin sauce and lime juice. Drizzle over the chicken wings. Before serving, sprinkle the wings with toasted sesame seeds and green onions, and mix to coat evenly.

For 5, 6 or 7 Crock-Pot® slow cooker, increase chicken wings to 5 lbs.

ZESTY ITALIAN BARBECUE MEATBALLS

Fresh homemade meatballs are the best, but if you're really pressed for time, use the frozen meatballs available at your local grocery store. Serve the meatballs with cocktail picks.

You may double the meatball ingredients for the 5, 6 or 7-quart Crock-Pot® slow cooker, but do not increase the sauce ingredients.

Meatballs:
2 lbs. ground beef
1 medium onion, finely chopped
1 cup bread crumbs
¼ cup fresh Italian parsley, minced
2 cloves garlic, minced
½ tsp. freshly ground black pepper
½ tsp. dry mustard
2 eggs, beaten

Sauce:
1½ cups bottled barbecue sauce
¾ cup tomato paste
⅓ cup ketchup
⅓ cup brown sugar
½ cup water, as needed
1 tsp. liquid smoke

In a mixing bowl, combine the meatball ingredients. Form into walnut-sized balls. Bake the meatballs in a shallow baking dish at 350°F for 20 minutes or until browned. Drain off any fat. Transfer meatballs to the Crock-Pot® slow cooker. In a separate mixing bowl, combine all sauce ingredients and mix thoroughly. Pour over the meatballs in the stoneware. Cover; cook on Low for 4 hours (or on High for 2 hours). Stir once in the middle of cooking to baste the meatballs with sauce. Remove the meatballs from the sauce to serve. Makes about 40 meatballs.

ARIZONA BLACK BEAN DIP

2–14 oz. cans black beans, drained
1 medium onion, finely diced
4 cloves garlic, minced
1 Tbs. ground cumin
1 tsp. cayenne pepper
14 oz. fresh goat cheese, crumbled (or any other fresh farmer's cheese)
¼ cup green onions, thinly sliced (reserve 1 Tbs. for garnish)
¼ cup fresh cilantro, chopped (reserve 1 Tbs. for garnish)
2 Tbs. pumpkin seeds, shelled and toasted, for garnish

This Southwest-inspired dip is given a twist with the addition of tangy goat cheese. The pumpkin seeds as garnish also give the dip a nice crunch. Serve with your favorite tortilla chips.

Combine all the ingredients in the Crock-Pot® slow cooker, except for the garnish ingredients. Cook on High 1½ to 2½ hours, or until the cheese has melted and is bubbly. Transfer to your serving dish and garnish the top with a sprinkling of green onions, cilantro, and pumpkin seeds.

For larger parties, you can double or even triple the recipe, using the 5, 6 or 7-quart Crock-Pot® slow cooker.

COUNTRY SCALLOPED POTATOES WITH HAM

The combination of the smoky flavor of the ham and the cream-iness of the potatoes create a homestyle feast. This can easily become a main entrée by increasing the proportion of the ham to the potatoes.

For the 5, 6 or 7-quart Crock-Pot® slow cooker, double all the ingredients except for the milk and butter.

6 medium potatoes, thinly sliced
15 thin slices country smoked ham
1 large onion, thinly sliced
1 cup cheddar cheese, shredded
¼ cup fresh Italian parsley, minced
10 button mushrooms, thinly sliced
½ cup milk
½ cup butter, melted
½ tsp. paprika
½ tsp. freshly ground black pepper
½ tsp. salt

Lightly grease the Crock-Pot® slow cooker. Alternate layers of potatoes, ham, onion, cheese, parsley and mushrooms in the stoneware. In a small bowl, combine the milk, butter, paprika, pepper, and salt. Pour this mixture over the layered ingredients in the slow cooker. Cover; cook on low for 7 to 9 hours (or on High for 3 to 4 hours). Makes 6 servings.

CREAMY CURRIED SPINACH

3–10 oz. packages frozen spinach, thawed
1 large onion, chopped
4 cloves garlic, minced
2 Tbs. curry powder
2 Tbs. butter or margarine, melted
¼ cup chicken stock
¼ cup heavy cream
1 tsp. lemon juice

The cream and butter of this recipe balance the intense flavoring imparted by the curry and garlic.

Combine the spinach, onion, garlic, curry powder, butter, and chicken stock in the Crock-Pot® slow cooker. Cover; cook on Low 3 to 4 hours (or on High for 2 hours). Thirty minutes before the end of the cooking time, add the heavy cream and lemon juice. Mix to combine. Replace the cover. Makes 8 servings.

For the 5, 6 or 7-quart Crock-Pot® slow cooker, double all ingredients except for the chicken stock and heavy cream.

FRESH VEGETABLE PAELLA

This side dish is a twist on the Spanish classic. You may also serve this as a main entrée.

5 oz. frozen chopped spinach, thawed and drained
2 cups converted white rice
4 cups vegetable stock
1 green bell pepper, seeded and chopped
1 medium tomato, sliced into wedges
1 medium onion, chopped
1 medium carrot, diced
3 cloves garlic, minced
1 Tbs. fresh Italian parsley, minced
1 tsp. saffron threads
1 tsp. salt
½ tsp. freshly ground black pepper
1–13¾ oz. can artichoke hearts, quartered, rinsed and well-drained
½ cup frozen peas

Combine the spinach, rice, vegetable stock, green pepper, tomato, onion, carrot, garlic, parsley, saffron, salt, and black pepper in the Crock-Pot® slow cooker. Mix thoroughly. Cover; cook on Low 4 hours (or on High for 2 hours). Add the artichoke hearts and peas to the paella 15 minutes prior to serving. Mix thoroughly to combine and replace the cover. Makes 8 side servings.

You may double all the ingredients for the 5, 6 or 7-quart Crock-Pot® slow cooker.

SUMMER VEGETABLE RATATOUILLE

This southern French classic is the perfect way to use those abundant, fresh summer vegetables.

2 medium eggplants, cut into ½-inch slices
salt
1 large onion, chopped
3 cloves garlic, minced
2 medium zucchini, cut into ½-inch slices
1 red pepper, seeded and chopped
1 medium yellow squash, cleaned and cut into ½-inch pieces
2 medium tomatoes, sliced into wedges
¼ cup olive oil
¼ cup dry white wine
1 Tbs. sugar
1 Tbs. red wine vinegar
¼ cup Parmesan cheese, grated

Place the eggplant slices in a large colander and sprinkle with salt to remove excess water. After 30 minutes, wash the salt off the eggplant and pat dry. In a medium skillet, lightly sauté the eggplant, onion, garlic, zucchini, and red pepper. Place the skillet ingredients in the Crock-Pot® slow cooker and add the squash, tomatoes, olive oil, wine, sugar and vinegar. Cover; cook on Low 4 to 6 hours (or on High for 2 to 3 hours). Sprinkle with Parmesan cheese before serving.

You may double all the ingredients, except the olive oil and wine, for the 5, 6 or 7-quart Crock-Pot® slow cooker.

GOLDEN ROASTED ROOT VEGETABLES

A great winter dish, you will enjoy this satisfying combination of the parsnips, carrots and Yukon Gold potatoes.

2 large parsnips, peeled and cut into ½-inch pieces
4 large carrots, peeled and cut into ½-inch pieces
6 medium Yukon Gold potatoes, peeled and cut into ½-inch pieces
1 Tbs. fresh tarragon, minced
1 Tbs. fresh sage, minced
¼ cup butter, melted
½ tsp. salt
½ tsp. pepper
1 tsp. brown sugar

Double all the ingredients for the 5, 6 or 7-quart Crock-Pot® slow cooker.

Combine all the ingredients in the Crock-Pot® slow cooker. Thoroughly coat the vegetables with the herbs, seasonings and butter. Cover; cook on Low 6 to 8 hours (or on High for 3 to 4 hours). Makes 6 side servings.

ROSEMARY RED JACKET POTATOES

10 to 12 medium red potatoes, cut into quarters
¼ cup fresh lemon juice
⅛ cup butter or margarine, melted
1 Tbs. extra virgin olive oil
3 cloves garlic, minced
2 Tbs. fresh rosemary leaves, minced
¾ tsp. salt
½ tsp. paprika
¼ cup fresh Italian parsley, chopped

A simple and elegant side dish for any meal.

Combine all of the ingredients except the parsley in the Crock-Pot® slow cooker. Make sure that the potatoes are evenly coated with the herbs and seasonings. Cover; cook on Low 6 to 8 hours (or on High 3 to 4 hours). Before serving, toss potatoes with the fresh parsley for added flavor and color. Makes 8 side servings.

You may double the ingredients for the 5, 6 or 7-quart Crock-Pot® slow cooker to make 16 servings.

CLASSIC CHEESE FONDUE

Dip skewered meats, vegetables, and bread into this delicious cheese fondue. Kirsch, a specialized brandy distilled from cherry juice, adds a hint of intense flavor to this party favorite. Kirsch is available in most supermarket liquor aisles.

For a 5, 6 or 7-quart Crock-Pot® slow cooker, double all ingredients.

2½ cups white wine
3 cloves garlic, finely minced
16 oz. Gruyere cheese, grated
1 lb. Swiss cheese, grated
3 Tbs. flour
3 Tbs. Kirsch
¼ tsp. ground nutmeg

In a large saucepan, heat the wine and garlic to a simmer. Combine the Gruyere and Swiss cheese and flour in a large bowl and slowly add the mixture to the wine. Stir constantly until the cheeses are completely integrated and melted. Add the Kirsch and stir. Pour the saucepan contents into the Crock-Pot® slow cooker and sprinkle with the nutmeg. Cover; cook on High 1 hour. Thoroughly mix the fondue, replace the cover and cook on Low for 2 hours. Makes enough fondue for 15 people as an appetizer.

RED ONION MARMALADE

5 large red onions, thinly sliced
4 Tbs. unsalted butter or margarine
1 Tbs. olive oil
2 cloves garlic, minced
½ tsp. ground cumin
½ tsp. ground coriander
½ tsp. salt
¼ cup water
2 Tbs. currant jelly

The natural sweetness of red onions highlights this recipe. Use the marmalade as a topping on steaks or fish, or spread the marmalade on toasted sourdough rounds as a savory and simple appetizer.

In a large skillet, carmelize the red onion in the olive oil, butter and garlic. Season with the cumin, coriander, salt and pepper. Transfer the marmalade to the Crock-Pot® slow cooker. Add the remaining ingredients and mix thoroughly. Cover; heat on High 1 hour. Allow the marmalade to cool before serving. The marmalade can be refrigerated for up to 4 days prior to serving.

You may double the onions, butter, oil, spices and jelly for the 5, 6 or 7-quart Crock-Pot® slow cooker.

FRUIT SKEWERS WITH APRICOT-GINGER DIPPING SAUCE

Use the season's freshest fruit to make this appetizer as colorful and flavorful as possible. Your guests will enjoy this fresh alternative to the typical fruit and cheese platter.

2 cups fresh or canned pineapple chunks
2 cups whole strawberries, de-stemmed
2 cups fresh melon of your choice, cut into bite-sized chunks
4 firm kiwi, peeled and cut into ½ inch pieces
skewers or toothpicks
2 Tbs. fresh ginger, grated
2 cups fresh or canned (drained) apricots, chopped
½ cup granulated sugar
3 cups whipped cream
¼ cup fresh mint leaves, minced
fresh mint sprigs, for garnish

To make fruit skewers, skewer fruit in alternating layers of color and sweetness. Or, simply skewer each piece of fruit with a toothpick. Skewers can be refrigerated up to 24 hours before serving. Makes enough skewers for about 15 people.

In the Crock-Pot® slow cooker, combine the ginger, apricots and sugar. Cover; cook on High 8 to 10 hours. Remove the cover during the last 30 minutes of cooking. Allow the apricot mixture to cool. Pour into a medium bowl and fold in the whipped cream and mint. Serve as a dipping sauce for the fruit skewers. Garnish the serving platter with fresh mint sprigs.

For a 5, 6 or 7-quart Crock-Pot® slow cooker, you may double all ingredients.

MANGO SPICED RIBS

Mango chutney adds sweetness and spice to these fall-off-the-bone beef ribs. Make sure to serve these with plenty of napkins!

3 lbs. beef short ribs
1 cup mango chutney
1 clove garlic, minced
1 Tbs. curry powder
½ tsp. cinnamon
½ tsp. salt

For the 5, 6 or 7-quart Crock-Pot® slow cooker, you may double all ingredients.

In a large skillet, brown the short ribs. Pour off the excess fat. In a small bowl, combine the chutney, garlic, curry powder, cinnamon and salt. Rub this mixture all over the ribs and place the ribs in the Crock-Pot® slow cooker. Drizzle any remaining chutney mixture over the ribs. Cover; cook on low for 6 to 8 hours (or on High for 3 to 4 hours). Makes 12 to 15 appetizer servings.

BRUNCH FLORENTINE

1½ cup cheddar cheese, grated and divided
1–9 oz. package frozen spinach, thawed and drained
1 cup white bread, cubed
1 cup fresh button mushrooms, sliced
½ cup green onions, thinly sliced
6 eggs
1½ cups milk
½ cup heavy cream
1 tsp. salt
1 tsp. freshly ground black pepper
1 tsp. garlic powder

Lightly grease the Crock-Pot® slow cooker. Layer half of the cheddar cheese, and spinach, bread, mushrooms and green onions in the bottom of the stoneware. In a medium mixing bowl, whisk together the eggs, milk, cream, salt, pepper and garlic powder until thoroughly combined. Pour this egg mixture over the layered mixture. Do not mix. Sprinkle the remaining cheese on top. Cover; cook on High 1½ to 2 hours. Makes 4 to 6 breakfast servings.

A decidedly elegant breakfast dish that is best accompanied by fresh fruit and muffins. This is a perfect entrée when hosting guests for brunch.

You may double all ingredients for the 5, 6 or 7-quart Crock-Pot® slow cooker.

HEARTY CHEESE HASH BROWNS

To transform this breakfast side dish to main course status, try adding 1½ cups diced ham to the recipe.

5 cups frozen hash brown potatoes
2 cups cheddar cheese, grated
1 cup milk
½ cup half-and-half
½ cup green onions, thinly sliced
1 cup frozen peas
1 tsp. salt
1 tsp. freshly ground black pepper
1 tsp. paprika

You may double all ingredients for the 5, 6 or 7-quart Crock-Pot® slow cooker.

Combine all ingredients in the Crock-Pot® slow cooker and mix thoroughly. Cover; cook on Low 6 to 8 hours (or on High for 3 to 4 hours). Makes 6 to 8 servings.

EASY ITALIAN SAUSAGE SCRAMBLE

1 medium onion, diced
1½ lbs. Italian sausage, removed from casing
6 medium red potatoes, diced
1 medium tomato, diced
1 cup fresh or frozen kernel corn
¼ cup fresh Italian parsley, minced
2 cups cheddar cheese, grated
1 cup milk
1½ tsp. salt
2 tsp. freshly ground black pepper

Choose your favorite style of Italian sausage to make this dish memorable or try a sweet or extra spicy style as an exciting variation.

In a medium skillet, sauté the onion and brown and crumble the sausage. Drain off any fat and transfer the sausage and onions to the Crock-Pot® slow cooker. Add the remaining ingredients, mixing well to combine thoroughly. Cover; cook on Low for 6 to 8 hours (or on High for 3 to 4 hours), or until the potatoes are tender. Makes 6 servings.

For the 5, 6 or 7-quart Crock-Pot® slow cooker, you may double all ingredients.

MIGAS

This breakfast dish of Southwest flavorings is an excellent way to use those leftover (and stale) tortilla chips. Serve with tortillas and refried beans for an authentic touch.

6 eggs
½ cup green onions, thinly sliced
½ cup red bell pepper, diced
1 cup Jack cheese, grated
1 cup cheddar cheese, grated
½ cup mild salsa
1 tsp. cumin
1 tsp. garlic powder
1 Tbs. fresh oregano, minced
½ cup milk
2½ cups salted tortilla chips, slightly broken up

You may double all the ingredients for the 5, 6 or 7-quart Crock-Pot® slow cooker.

Combine all the ingredients in the Crock-Pot® slow cooker. Mix thoroughly. Cover; cook on Low 4 to 6 hours (or on High for 2 to 3 hours). Makes 6 servings.

FRESH VEGETABLE & THREE-CHEESE FRITTATA

1 cup zucchini, thinly sliced
1 cup yellow squash, thinly sliced
½ cup red pepper, seeded and diced
2 cloves garlic, minced
1 cup asparagus, cut into1-inch pieces
8 large eggs
½ cup fontina cheese, grated
½ cup mozzarella cheese, grated
½ cup Parmesan cheese, grated
¼ cup fresh Italian parsley, minced
1 tsp. salt
1 tsp. freshly ground black pepper

In a medium skillet, sauté the zucchini, yellow squash, red pepper and garlic until tender. Transfer the vegetables to the Crock-Pot® slow cooker and add the remaining ingredients, mixing thoroughly to combine. Cover; cook on Low 4 to 6 hours (or on High for 2 to 3 hours). Makes 6 servings.

Full of fresh vegetables, this Italian-style breakfast dish is a great alternative for vegetarians. Round out the meal with toast, fresh fruit, and steaming cups of Italian espresso.

For the 5, 6 or 7-quart Crock-Pot® slow cooker, double all ingredients.

41

CHAPTER 3

HEARTY CROCK-POT®
SLOW COOKER BEEF,
PORK & LAMB RECIPES

Slow cooking is the ideal way to release intense and succulent flavors from beef, pork, and lamb. Not only will your Crock-Pot® slow cooker make these meats incredibly tender and juicy, but your preparation of such dishes will be amazingly simple. Most of the recipes included in this chapter require very few preparatory steps. Just a few minutes of effort in the morning will result in a fabulous meal waiting for you at dinnertime.

Included in this chapter are traditional dishes such as French Beef Burgundy, Beef & Button Mushroom Stroganoff, Pork Loin with Sherry and Onions, and Grandmother's Stuffed Bell Peppers. The Crock-Pot® slow cooker is an exemplary way to create these classics with a minimum of fuss and effort, but with a maximum of luscious taste.

We have also taken some classic recipes in this chapter and given them a flavorful twist. The typical meatloaf is brought to new heights with a flavorful and savory stuffing. Pork chops are given new life with a bit of sweetness and spice. Lamb shanks with a Middle Eastern slant are fall-off-the-bone tender. Be daring and exercise your own culinary creativity. Create new favorites from old stand-bys by adding fresh, seasonal herbs and vegetables and even fruit. Don't be afraid to experiment!

WILD MUSHROOM BEEF STEW

This classic beef stew is given a twist with the addition of flavorful shiitake mushrooms. If shiitake mushrooms are unavailable in your local grocery store, you can substitute other mushrooms of your choice. For extra punch, add a few dried porcini mushrooms to the stew.

You may double the amount of meat, mushrooms, carrots, potatoes, onion and celery for the 5, 6 or 7-quart Crock-Pot® slow cooker.

1½ to 2 lbs. beef stew meat, cut in 1-inch cubes
⅛ cup flour
½ tsp. salt
½ tsp. pepper
1½ cups beef broth
1 tsp. Worcestershire sauce
1 clove garlic, minced

1 bay leaf
1 tsp. paprika
4 shiitake mushrooms, sliced
2 medium carrots, sliced
2 medium potatoes, diced
1 small white onion, chopped
1 stalk celery, sliced

Put the beef in the Crock-Pot® slow cooker. Mix together the flour, salt and pepper, and pour over the meat; stirring to coat each piece of meat with flour. Add the remaining ingredients and stir to mix well. Cover; cook on Low 10 to 12 hours (or on High for 4 to 6 hours). Stir the stew thoroughly before serving. Makes 5 servings.

SUNDAY DINNER BEEF ROAST

3 to 4 lb. rump, pot, or chuck roast
2 cloves garlic, sliced
1 tsp. freshly ground pepper
1 tsp. salt
½ cup white wine
3 medium potatoes, chopped
2 large carrots, sliced
1 onion, chopped
1 tsp. fresh parsley, minced
1 tsp. fresh rosemary, leaves only
1 tsp. fresh thyme, minced

Using a small knife, make several slits all over the roast. Insert slices of garlic into these slits. Rub the outside of the roast with the salt and pepper. Place in the Crock-Pot® slow cooker and add the remaining ingredients. Cover; cook on Low 10 to 12 hours (or on High for 5 to 6 hours). Remove the roast and let it rest for 15 minutes before slicing. Makes 10 to 12 servings.

To make this meal more elegant, use new potatoes, baby carrots and pearl onions, instead of the cut-up vegetables.

For the 5, 6 or 7-quart Crock-Pot® slow cooker, prepare a 5 to 7 lb. roast and double the amount of seasoning, potatoes, carrots and onion.

ITALIAN-STYLE ROAST

Accented by amazing Italian herbs and flavorings, this succulent roast is drizzled with a rich tomato sauce and is best served over rice or pasta.

1–6 oz. can tomato paste
2 cloves garlic, minced
1 pkg. dry onion soup mix
2 tsp. fresh oregano, chopped
2 tsp. fresh thyme, chopped
1 tsp. salt
1 tsp. freshly ground black pepper
2 lbs. chuck roast, trimmed of any
    excess fat

1–16 oz. can tomatoes, drained
    and chopped
1 medium onion, chopped
2 medium carrots, chopped
1 medium potato, chopped
1 large celery stalk, sliced
2 bay leaves

You may double all the ingredients for the 5, 6 or 7-quart Crock-Pot® slow cooker.

In a small mixing bowl, combine the tomato paste, garlic, onion soup mix, oregano, thyme, salt and pepper. Rub this mixture all over the chuck roast and place the roast in the Crock-Pot® slow cooker. Add the remaining ingredients and any leftover tomato sauce. Cover; cook on Low 8 to 10 hours (or on High for 4 to 5 hours). Makes 6 servings.

FRENCH BEEF BURGUNDY

¼ cup all-purpose flour

½ tsp. salt

½ tsp. freshly ground black pepper

2 lbs. boneless beef chuck, cut into 1-inch cubes

2 Tbs. olive oil

1 medium onion, sliced

8 button mushrooms, sliced

½ cup fresh parsley, minced

3 cloves garlic, minced

2 bay leaves

1 cup burgundy wine

½ cup beef broth

Combine the flour, salt and black pepper. Dredge the beef cubes in the flour mixture, and brown in the olive oil in a medium skillet. Place the beef and remaining ingredients in the Crock-Pot® slow cooker and mix thoroughly to combine. Cover; cook on Low 4 to 6 hours (or on High for 2 to 3 hours). Makes 6 servings.

Burgundy wine imparts a hearty flavor to this French country stew. Serve over broad noodles for a perfect family meal.

For the 5, 6 or 7-quart Crock-Pot® slow cooker, double all ingredients.

SPINACH & FETA-STUFFED MEATLOAF

This tasty version of the traditional meatloaf reveals a delicious spinach-feta stuffing.

2 lbs. ground beef

2 large eggs

⅔ cup seasoned bread crumbs

1 package dry onion soup mix

2 cloves garlic, minced

¼ cup Parmesan cheese, grated

½ cup ketchup

¾ cup feta cheese, crumbled

3 Tbs. sun-dried tomatoes, minced

1–10 oz. package frozen chopped spinach, thawed and squeezed dry

Reserve 2 tablespoons of ketchup. In a large bowl, combine the ground beef, eggs, bread crumbs, onion soup mix, garlic, Parmesan cheese and remaining ketchup. In a small bowl, mix together the feta cheese and sun-dried tomatoes. On a cutting board covered with wax paper, pat the meat mixture into a rectangle, approximately 6" x 10." Spread the feta cheese mixture over the meat rectangle to within 1-inch of the edges. Place the spinach over the feta. Using the wax paper, roll the meat loaf so that the meat completely covers the cheese and spinach center. Make sure that the ends of the meat loaf are also completely sealed. Place in the Crock-Pot® slow cooker, on one end, if necessary. Top with the remaining ketchup. Cover; cook on Low 8 to 10 hours (or on High for 4 to 6 hours).

For the 5, 6 or 7-quart Crock-Pot® slow cooker, increase the eggs to 3 and the ketchup to ¾ cup and double all remaining ingredients.

BEEF & BUTTON MUSHROOM STROGANOFF

For a change of pace, try chicken or pork in this recipe.

3 lbs. boneless sirloin or beef round steak, cut into thin strips
½ cup flour
2 tsp. salt
1 tsp. freshly ground black pepper
2 medium onions, thinly sliced into rings
20 fresh button mushrooms, sliced
1½ cups beef broth
¼ cup dry white wine
1 tsp. Worcestershire sauce
1½ cups sour cream
¼ cup flour
4 cups egg noodles, cooked and drained
2 Tbs. fresh parsley, minced

Dredge the beef strips in the flour, salt and pepper. Place the coated beef strips in the Crock-Pot® slow cooker. Add the onions, mushrooms, beef broth, wine, and Worcestershire sauce. Cover; cook on Low 8 to 10 hours (or on High for 4 to 5 hours). Before serving, combine the sour cream and flour thoroughly, and add to the stoneware contents. Mix well and let cook for a further 10 minutes. Serve over the egg noodles. Garnish with the parsley.

For the 5, 6 or 7-quart Crock-Pot® slow cooker, double all ingredients except for beef broth, white wine, sour cream, and flour. Increase sour cream to 2½ cups, and flour to ½ cup.

SUMMERTIME BEEF & GARDEN VEGETABLE SALAD

A light and intensely flavorful salad entrée. Serve with warm, crusty bread for a perfect summer evening meal.

1 lb. beef flank steak, visible fat removed
3 Tbs. soy sauce
2 Tbs. oil
2 Tbs. honey
2 Tbs. garlic, finely chopped
1 tsp. ground ginger
2 Tbs. green onions, chopped

10 cups romaine lettuce greens, washed and torn
1 cup cherry tomatoes, halved
1 cucumber, peeled and thinly sliced
2 ribs celery, washed and diced
¼ tsp. freshly ground black pepper

Place the steak in the Crock-Pot® slow cooker (cut in half, if necessary, to fit). In a small bowl, combine the soy sauce, oil, honey, garlic, ground ginger and green onions. Mix well and pour over the steak. Cover and cook on Low for 8 to 10 hours (or on High for 3 to 4 hours). Transfer the steak to a carving platter and slice the steak thinly across the grain of the meat. Reserve the marinade.

To assemble the salad, toss the lettuce, tomatoes, cucumber and celery in a large serving bowl. Place the beef slices on top of the salad, drizzle with the warm marinade and toss again. Divide the salad onto individual plates, dust each salad with black pepper and serve immediately. Serves 4.

For the 5, 6 or 7-quart Crock-Pot® slow cooker, double all ingredients.

ANY DAY OF THE WEEK BEEF CHILI

Deliciously spicy, this chili's heat quotient can be increased by the addition of more cayenne pepper and canned green chilies.

2 medium onions, chopped

4 cloves garlic, minced

2 green bell peppers, chopped

2 lbs. ground chuck beef

2–14 oz. cans pinto beans, drained

1–14 oz. can tomatoes, drained and chopped

1–4 oz. can green chilies, chopped

1 Tbs. dried oregano

2 tsp. ground cumin

1 tsp. cayenne pepper

1 tsp. freshly ground black pepper

1 tsp. salt

1 cup beef or chicken broth

1 cup sour cream

1 cup sharp cheddar cheese, grated

2 Tbs. green onions, thinly sliced

In a large skillet, sauté the onions, garlic, and bell peppers until soft. Brown the ground chuck and drain off any excess fat. Transfer the meat and vegetables to the Crock-Pot® slow cooker. Add the oregano, cumin, cayenne pepper, black pepper, salt and broth. Mix thoroughly. Cover; cook on Low 6 to 8 hours (or on High for 3 to 4 hours). To serve, ladle the chili into individual bowls and garnish each with sour cream, cheddar cheese and green onions. Makes 6 to 8 servings.

For the 5, 6 or 7-quart Crock-Pot® slow cooker, double all ingredients.

TANGERINE BROCCOLI BEEF

Tender beef meets vegetables and tangerines in a tangy Oriental sauce.

1½ lbs. boneless beef top sirloin steak, cut into thin strips

1 red bell pepper, seeded and sliced into strips

2 cloves garlic, minced

1 Tbs. fresh ginger, grated

½ tsp. crushed red pepper

1 Tbs. soy sauce

2 Tbs. rice vinegar

1 Tbs. oyster sauce

¼ cup dry sherry

2 cups broccoli flowerets

1½ Tbs. cornstarch

2 Tbs. water

2 cans tangerine segments, drained

½ cup green onions, thinly sliced

4 cups sticky white rice

For 5, 6 or 7-quart Crock-Pot® slow cooker, double all ingredients.

Combine the steak, bell pepper, garlic, ginger, red pepper, soy sauce, rice vinegar, oyster sauce and sherry in the Crock-Pot® slow cooker. Cover; cook on Low 8 to 10 hours (or on High for 4 to 5 hours). During the last 30 minutes of cooking, add the broccoli flowerets and mix to combine. Combine the cornstarch and water in a small bowl and add to the juice in the stoneware. This will thicken the juices to make the sauce. Replace the cover and finish cooking. When done cooking, toss the steak mixture with the tangerine segments and green onions. Serve over white rice. Makes 6 servings.

GRANDMOTHER'S STUFFED PEPPERS

6 tall green bell peppers, hollowed
1½ lbs. ground beef
1 medium onion, chopped
1 medium carrot, diced
1 large tomato, diced
1 cup fresh or frozen corn kernels
1 cup cooked rice
1 cup ketchup

2 cloves garlic, minced
1 tsp. salt
1 tsp. freshly ground black pepper
1 Tbs. fresh oregano, minced
2 Tbs. fresh Italian parsley, minced
1–10¾ oz. can condensed tomato soup

Fresh vegetables partner with beef and peppers in a delightful tomato sauce.

In a large mixing bowl, combine all the ingredients except for the bell peppers and tomato soup. Stuff each bell pepper with this mixture and place the peppers side-by-side in the Crock-Pot® slow cooker. Pour the tomato soup over the peppers. Cover; cook on Low 6 to 8 hours (or on High for 3 to 4 hours).

You may increase the recipe ingredients, except the tomato soup, for the 5, 6 or 7-quart Crock-Pot® slow cooker, however the peppers should fit comfortably in a single layer in your stoneware.

TRADITIONAL CORNED BEEF & CABBAGE

A simple and classic dish that leaves your stomach feeling satisfied.

6 small new potatoes, quartered
2 medium carrots, thickly sliced
1½ to 2 lb. corned beef brisket
1 medium onion, cut into eighths
3 bay leaves
8 whole black peppercorns
½ head cabbage, cored and cut into wedges

For 5, 6 or 7-quart Crock-Pot slow cooker, double all the ingredients, except for the bay leaves and black peppercorns.

Place the potatoes and carrots in the bottom of the Crock-Pot® slow cooker. Cover with the beef brisket, and place the onion, bay leaves, and peppercorns on top. Add water to cover. Cover; cook on Low 8 to 10 hours (or on High for 4 to 5 hours). Halfway through cooking, add the cabbage wedges. Makes 5 servings.

PORK LOIN WITH SHERRY AND RED ONIONS

3 large red onions, thinly sliced
1 cup pearl onions, blanched and peeled
2 Tbs. unsalted butter or margarine
½ tsp. salt
½ tsp. freshly ground black pepper
2½ lb. boneless pork loin, tied
½ cup cooking sherry
2 Tbs. Italian parsley, chopped

1½ Tbs. cornstarch
2 Tbs. water

In a medium skillet, sauté the red onions and pearl onions in the butter until soft. Season with salt and pepper. Rub the pork loin with salt and pepper and place in the Crock-Pot® slow cooker. Add the sautéed onions, sherry and parsley. Cover; cook on Low 8 to 10 hours (or on High for 5 to 6 hours). Remove the pork loin from the stoneware and let stand 15 minutes before slicing. Combine the cornstarch and water and add to the juice in the stoneware to thicken the sauce. Serve the pork loin with the onions and sherry sauce. Makes 8 servings.

The mild flavor of pork is awakened by this rich, delectable sauce.

If using the 5, 6 or 7-quart Crock-Pot® slow cooker, double all ingredients, except for the sherry, cornstarch and water.

CARIBBEAN PORK CHOPS

These pork chops get their spice from the Scotch Bonnet chile pepper, one of the hottest chile peppers available, often used in Caribbean cooking. If a Scotch Bonnet is unavailable, use a Habañero chile pepper. Use care while seeding and chopping the chile to avoid getting the fiery oil on your hands or in your eyes.

You may double all ingredients for the 5, 6 or 7-quart Crock-Pot® slow cooker.

1 tsp. ground allspice
1 tsp. freshly ground black pepper
1 tsp. ground cinnamon
½ tsp. ground nutmeg
2 tsp. dried thyme
½ cup scallions, finely chopped
3 Tbs. soy sauce
2 Tbs. fresh ginger, grated

1 Scotch Bonnet (or Habañero) chile pepper, seeded and minced
2 Tbs. garlic, minced
2 tsp. sugar
1 tsp. salt
4 lean pork chops, 1-inch thick

In a food processor, combine all of the herbs and spices with the scallions, soy sauce, fresh ginger, chile pepper, garlic, sugar and salt, and process to a coarse paste. Coat the pork chops with this paste and place in the Crock-Pot® slow cooker. Cover; cook on Low 7 to 9 hours (or on High for 4 to 5 hours). Makes 4 servings.

POLYNESIAN PORK ROAST

¼ cup soy sauce

1 tsp. liquid smoke

1–20 oz. can crushed pineapple, drained

¼ cup fresh orange juice

¼ cup fresh lemon juice

1 Tbs. orange zest, grated

1 Tbs. lemon zest, grated

3 Tbs. sugar

2 Tbs. cornstarch

3 lb. boneless pork shoulder roast (Boston butt)

Pineapple and citrus flavors give this pork roast sweet and mellow undertones. Serve with white rice and a fresh green salad for a satisfying meal.

In a medium saucepan, combine the soy sauce, liquid smoke, pineapple, orange juice, lemon juice, orange zest, lemon zest and sugar. Bring mixture to a boil and add the cornstarch, stirring constantly until thickened. Place the pork roast in the Crock-Pot® slow cooker and pour half of the fruit glaze over the roast. Reserve the remaining glaze. Cover the slow cooker; cook on Low 8 to 10 hours (or on High for 4 to 5 hours). Warm the remaining glaze on low heat and serve over the pork. Makes 8 servings.

For the 5, 6 or 7-quart Crock-Pot® slow cooker, double all ingredients except the cornstarch. Increase the cornstarch to 3 Tbs.

CRANBERRY-MUSTARD PORK TENDERLOIN

An exquisite combination of cranberry and mustard bestows a tangy flavor to the pork tenderloin. Serve with cranberry sauce on the side for an unusual, but flavorful holiday entrée.

1–16 oz. can whole berry cranberry sauce
3 Tbs. fresh lemon juice
4 Tbs. Dijon mustard
3 Tbs. brown sugar
2 pork tenderloins (about 2 lbs. total)

For 5, 6 or 7-quart Crock-Pot® slow cooker, double all ingredients.

In a small mixing bowl, combine the cranberry sauce, lemon juice, mustard and brown sugar. Spread this mixture over the pork tenderloins and place them in the Crock-Pot® slow cooker. Pour the remaining cranberry mixture over the tenderloins. Cover; cook on Low 8 to 10 hours (or on High for 4 to 5 hours). Makes 6 servings.

LAMB SHANK TANGINE

4 lamb shanks

2 medium carrots, cut into ½-inch slices

1 large onion, diced

4 Tbs. ginger, grated

6 cloves garlic, roughly chopped

2 Tbs. ground cumin

1 Tbs. ground cinnamon

1 cup black raisins

1 cup black olives

3 cups chicken stock

¼ cup fresh lemon juice

1 Tbs. sugar

1 tsp. salt

1 tsp. freshly ground pepper

These succulent lamb shanks will fall apart at the bone and are bathed in a savory sweet broth. Serve with couscous and a fresh green salad.

In a large skillet, quickly brown the lamb shanks. Remove the lamb shanks from the skillet. In the same skillet, sauté the carrots, onions, ginger and garlic. Add the spices to awaken their aroma. In the Crock-Pot® slow cooker, combine the lamb shanks, sautéed mixture, raisins, olives, chicken stock, lemon juice, sugar, salt and pepper. Cover; cook on Low 8 to 10 hours (or on High for 4 to 5 hours). Makes 4 servings.

You may double all ingredients, except the chicken stock and lemon juice, for the 5, 6 or 7-quart Crock-Pot® slow cooker.

STUFFED LAMB ROAST

The addition of lemon zest brightens the flavors of the stuffing for this lovely lamb roast.

3 lb. lamb roast, deboned
1 medium onion, finely chopped
⅛ cup unsalted butter or
    margarine, softened
½ cup unseasoned bread crumbs
1 egg, beaten
1 tsp. salt
1 tsp. freshly ground black pepper

1 Tbs. fresh rosemary, minced
1 Tbs. fresh mint, minced
1 Tbs. lemon zest, grated
1 Tbs. extra virgin olive oil
3 cloves garlic, minced
2 stalks celery, thinly sliced
1 medium carrot, finely chopped
salt and pepper to taste

You may double all ingredients when using the 5, 6 or 7-quart Crock-Pot® slow cooker.

Remove excess fat from the lamb roast. In a medium mixing bowl, combine the remaining ingredients to form a stuffing. Stuff the lamb with this mixture. Roll the lamb and fasten with skewers or string and season with salt and pepper. Place the roast in the Crock-Pot® slow cooker and cook on High for 1 hour, then turn to Low for 10 to 12 hours. Let the lamb rest for 15 minutes before slicing. Pour the natural juices over the roast to serve. Makes 8 servings.

LAMB CHOPS WITH RED WINE GLAZE

6 lamb rib chops

2 Tbs. vegetable oil

2 cups brown cremini mushrooms, sliced
    (or portabellas, if available)

½ cup red wine, preferably Merlot

2 tsp. salt

2 cloves garlic, minced

1 Tbs. honey

1 tsp. dried marjoram

1 tsp. dried oregano

1 tsp. dried basil

When cooking with wine, select a high quality wine that would be equally enjoyable to drink. A delicious Merlot wine splendidly accents the rich qualities of the lamb and mushrooms in this dish.

In a large skillet, brown the lamb chops in the vegetable oil. Drain well. Sauté the mushrooms to remove as much moisture as possible. In a small mixing bowl, whisk together the red wine, salt, garlic, honey, marjoram, oregano and basil. Combine all the ingredients in the Crock-Pot® slow cooker, making sure the lamb chops are well-coated with the wine mixture. Cover; cook on Low for 6 to 8 hours (or on High for 3 to 4 hours). Serve the lamb chops with the mushrooms and wine sauce on top. Makes 6 servings.

For 5, 6 or 7-quart Crock-Pot® slow cooker, double all ingredients.

CHAPTER 4

TEMPTING CROCK-POT®
SLOW COOKER CHICKEN
& TURKEY DISHES

Poultry is a family favorite because it is versatile, inexpensive, healthy and delicious. Chicken and turkey can be paired with almost anything and are most likely to appear on your dinner menu. It is often on sale at your grocery store and is among the lowest fat and highest protein choices (once the skin has been removed). In addition, both chicken and turkey are full of satisfying flavor.

However, it is easy to fall into a rut with poultry, cooking the same chicken and turkey dishes over and over again. To avoid this common problem, we have included recipes that exploit the versatility of poultry, but also exercise culinary creativity. Unusual, but delicious, combinations of spices and flavorings with slow-cooking can bring out the best in poultry, as our recipes clearly show. Not only will these dishes tantalize your tastebuds, but they can also be elegantly presented and served to guests, should the occasion require. And most importantly, they are Crock-Pot® slow cooker dishes so they are easy to prepare and easy to clean up. Just add the ingredients into the slow cooker and go!

In addition to these more daring dishes, we have also included those traditional dishes that your family loves. Classic combinations of herbs, lemon, and other flavorings always accent chicken and turkey quite well. Sometimes "down home" recipes cannot be beat, and the slow cooker is the perfect vehicle to highlight your homestyle cooking.

SAVORY CHICKEN CHILI

Also called "white" chili, this bean stew is a combination of chicken, white beans, and Southwest seasonings. Serve with cheese quesadillas.

3–15 oz. cans great northern or cannellini beans, drained
2 cups cooked chicken, chopped
1 medium onion, chopped
2 medium red peppers, seeded and chopped
1–4 oz. can diced green chilies
3 cloves garlic, minced
3½ cups chicken broth
2 tsp. ground cumin
1 tsp. salt
1 tsp. dried oregano

You may double all ingredients when using a 5, 6 or 7-quart Crock-Pot® slow cooker.

Combine all ingredients in the Crock-Pot® slow cooker. Mix thoroughly. Cover; cook on Low 8 to 10 hours (or on High for 4 to 5 hours). Makes 8 servings.

HERBED GARLIC CHICKEN

⅛ cup butter or margarine, softened
8 cloves garlic, minced
1 Tbs. fresh rosemary leaves, chopped
½ tsp. salt
½ tsp. freshly ground pepper
1–3 lb. whole chicken, cleaned
1 cup chicken broth
3 Tbs. fresh lemon juice
6 small red potatoes, halved
2 Tbs. chives, minced, for garnish

This simple chicken entrée is infused with garlic and herbs.

In a small mixing bowl, combine the butter, garlic, rosemary, salt and pepper until well incorporated. Rub this compound butter under and over the skin of the chicken and in the cavity. Place the chicken, chicken broth, lemon juice and potatoes in the Crock-Pot® slow cooker. Cover; heat on Low 8 to 10 hours (or on High for 3½ to 5 hours). Remove the chicken and potatoes with a spatula. Garnish with the chives. Makes 4 servings.

For the 5, 6 or 7-quart Crock-Pot® slow cooker, double all ingredients, except for the lemon juice.

ROAST CHICKEN WITH PEAS, PROSCIUTTO AND CREAM

This sophisticated dish is surprisingly simple to make. The rustic taste of the prosciutto or bacon beautifully balances the creaminess of this chicken entrée.

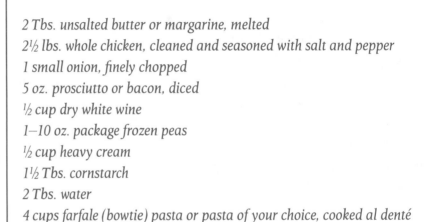

2 Tbs. unsalted butter or margarine, melted
2½ lbs. whole chicken, cleaned and seasoned with salt and pepper
1 small onion, finely chopped
5 oz. prosciutto or bacon, diced
½ cup dry white wine
1–10 oz. package frozen peas
½ cup heavy cream
1½ Tbs. cornstarch
2 Tbs. water
4 cups farfale (bowtie) pasta or pasta of your choice, cooked al denté

You may double all the ingredients, except the wine and cream, and use a 5, 6 or 7-quart Crock-Pot® slow cooker.

Combine the chicken, onion, prosciutto and wine in the Crock-Pot® slow cooker. Cover; cook on Low 8 to 10 hours (or on High for 3½ to 4 hours). In the last 30 minutes of cooking, add the frozen peas and heavy cream to the liquid in the stoneware. After cooking, remove the chicken from the stoneware and carve the meat in slices. Combine the cornstarch and water and add to the juice in the Crock-Pot® slow cooker to thicken the sauce. To serve, spoon the pasta onto individual plates, place the chicken over the pasta and top each portion with sauce. Makes 6 servings.

GREEN TOMATILLO CHICKEN

6 boneless, skinless chicken breasts
1 medium onion, sliced
2 cloves garlic, minced
1 tsp. ground cumin
1 tsp. dried oregano
1 tsp. salt
1 tsp. freshly ground pepper
1 Tbs. fresh lemon juice
1 cup green tomatillo salsa
1½ cups sour cream

This exceptional dish pairs chicken with a creamy tomatillo sauce. Serve with Spanish rice and earthy, roasted vegetables for a beautiful meal.

Place the chicken breasts in the Crock-Pot® slow cooker. In a small mixing bowl, combine the onion, garlic, cumin, oregano, salt, pepper, lemon juice and salsa. Pour this sauce over the chicken breasts. Cook on Low 6 to 8 hours (or on High for 3 to 4 hours). Remove the chicken from the slow cooker. Stir the sour cream into the juices in the stoneware and blend well. Pour this sauce over each piece of chicken. Makes 6 servings.

For the 5, 6 or 7-quart Crock-Pot® slow cooker, double all ingredients.

HONEY HOISIN CHICKEN

This sweet and savory chicken dish goes well with a broccoli or asparagus side dish.

6 whole boneless, skinless chicken breasts
3 Tbs. soy sauce
3 Tbs. honey
3 Tbs. hoisin sauce
2 Tbs. dry white wine
1 Tbs. fresh ginger, grated
1 tsp. freshly ground black pepper
2 Tbs. sesame seeds, toasted
6 cups prepared, hot white rice

You may double all the ingredients when using the 5, 6 or 7-quart Crock-Pot® slow cooker.

Combine all ingredients in the Crock-Pot® slow cooker. Cover; cook on Low 4 to 6 hours (or on High for 2 to 3 hours). Halfway through cooking, turn the chicken breasts in the sauce to thoroughly re-coat. Once cooked, remove the chicken from the sauce and carve the chicken into slices. Serve over fluffy, hot white rice. Sprinkle with the toasted sesame seeds. Makes 6 servings.

APRICOT MUSTARD CHICKEN

1–11½ oz. can apricot juice/nectar
2 Tbs. Dijon mustard
1 clove garlic, minced
¼ tsp. fresh ginger, grated
¼ tsp. cayenne pepper
⅛ tsp. ground allspice
⅛ tsp. turmeric
⅛ tsp. ground cardamom
6 boneless, skinless chicken breasts
4 cups prepared couscous or wild rice

In a mixing bowl, whisk together the apricot nectar, mustard, garlic, ginger and spices. Dip each chicken breast in the apricot mixture and put in Crock-Pot® slow cooker. Pour the remaining sauce over the breasts. Cover; cook on Low 7 to 9 hours (or on High for 4 to 5 hours). Remove the chicken from the stoneware and arrange over rice or couscous. Pour the apricot sauce over the chicken breasts. Makes 6 servings.

The piquancy of the spices is tempered by the sweetness of the apricot juice… a perfect combination to highlight the chicken breasts.

For a 5, 6 or 7-quart Crock-Pot® slow cooker, double all ingredients.

CHICKEN PROVENÇAL

This Southern French chicken dish contrasts the citrus with the sweet. Serve with a crusty French baguette and seasonal vegetables.

2 lbs. skinless, boneless chicken thighs, each cut into quarters
2 medium red peppers, cut into ¼-inch thick slices
1 medium yellow pepper, cut into ¼-inch thick slices
1 onion, thinly sliced
1–28 oz. can plum tomatoes, drained
3 cloves garlic, minced
¼ tsp. salt
¼ tsp. dried thyme
¼ tsp. fennel seeds, crushed
3 strips orange peel
½ cup fresh basil leaves, chopped

You may double all the ingredients when using a 5, 6 or 7-quart Crock-Pot® slow cooker.

Place all the ingredients in the Crock-Pot® slow cooker, except for basil leaves. Mix thoroughly. Cover; cook on Low 7 to 9 hours (or on High for 3 to 4 hours). Sprinkle with the fresh basil to serve. Makes 8 servings.

CHICKEN CORDON BLEU ROLLS

6 chicken breasts, pounded to 1/4-inch thickness
6 pieces prosciutto
6 slices Swiss cheese
salt and pepper to taste
1/2 can (10 1/2 oz.) cream of mushroom soup
1/4 cup milk
1/4 cup white wine

These delicious rolls are easy to make, yet will impress your most discerning guests. Serve with wild rice and asparagus for an elegant meal.

On each chicken breast, place one piece of prosciutto and cheese. Roll up each chicken breast and secure with a toothpick. Season each roll with salt and pepper. Place in the Crock-Pot® slow cooker. In a small bowl, whisk together the soup, milk and white wine. Pour this mixture over the chicken breast rolls. Cover; cook on Low 4 to 6 hours (or on High for 3 to 4 hours). Makes 6 servings.

You may double the chicken breasts, prosciutto and Swiss cheese when using a 5, 6 or 7-quart Crock-Pot® slow cooker.

PESTO-STUFFED CHICKEN BREASTS

The fresh flavor of basil highlights an entrée that is the centerpiece of a summer feast. And, any leftover chicken is perfect as a filling for a delicious sandwich the next day.

You may double the chicken breasts, ricotta, Parmesan and pesto when using a 5, 6 or 7-quart Crock-Pot® slow cooker.

1 cup ricotta cheese
¼ cup Parmesan cheese
½ cup pesto sauce
6 chicken breasts, pounded out thin
salt and pepper
½ can (10½ oz.) cream of mushroom soup
¼ cup milk
¼ cup white wine
toasted pine nuts, for garnish
fresh basil leaves, for garnish

In a small mixing bowl, combine the ricotta, pesto and Parmesan cheese. Place a dollop of the pesto-ricotta mixture on each chicken breast. Roll up each chicken breast and secure with a toothpick. Season each roll with salt and pepper. Place in the Crock-Pot® slow cooker. In a small bowl, whisk together the soup, milk and white wine. Pour this mixture over the chicken breast rolls. Cover; cook on Low 4 to 6 hours (or on High for 3 to 4 hours). Garnish each chicken breast with toasted pine nuts and fresh basil leaves. Makes 6 servings.

CURRIED APPLE CHICKEN

6 boneless, skinless chicken breasts, cut into bite-sized pieces
1½ cups plain croutons
½ cup apple juice
1 tsp. salt
1 tsp. freshly ground black pepper
½ cup celery, sliced
½ cup raisins
1 large cooking apple, chopped
½ cup onion, chopped
2 tsp. brown sugar
2 tsp. curry powder

Place the chicken breasts in the Crock-Pot® slow cooker. Combine the remaining ingredients in a mixing bowl and spoon over the chicken breasts. Cover; cook on Low 6 to 8 hours (or on High for 3 to 4 hours). Makes 6 servings.

An appetizing combination of chicken and spice, tempered by the sweetness of apples.

To increase the quantity for a 5, 6 or 7-quart Crock-Pot® slow cooker, double all the ingredients, except the apple juice. Increase the juice to ¾ cup.

CHICKEN AND VEGETABLE LASAGNE

This lasagne combines a white sauce and chicken to lighten the flavors of this typically heavy Italian dish. You may substitute the season's freshest vegetables for the zucchini and carrots. Serve the lasagne with bruschetta and a tomato salad for a delightful meal.

1 large onion, chopped

1 medium zucchini, diced

1 medium carrot, diced

2 cloves garlic, minced

2½ cups cooked chicken, shredded

1 Tbs. fresh oregano, minced

2 Tbs. fresh Italian parsley, minced

1 Tbs. fresh thyme, minced

1 tsp. salt

1 tsp. freshly ground black pepper

1–10 oz. package broad lasagne noodles, cooked al denté, drained and cut into thirds

White Sauce

2 Tbs. butter or margarine, melted

2 Tbs. all-purpose flour

1 tsp. salt

1 cup milk

2 cups shredded mozzarella cheese, divided

1–12 oz. carton cottage cheese

In a medium skillet, sauté the onion, zucchini, carrot and garlic until tender. Add the chicken and season with the oregano, parsley, thyme, salt and pepper. Transfer the chicken and vegetables to the Crock-Pot® slow cooker. Add the lasagne noodles. In a medium mixing bowl, combine the butter, flour, salt, milk, 1 cup of the mozzarella cheese and the cottage cheese to make the White Sauce. Stir the sauce into the chicken and vegetables in the stoneware. Cover; cook on Low 4 to 6 hours (or on High for 2 to 3 hours). During the last 30 minutes of cooking, top the lasagne with the remaining mozzarella cheese and turn to High. Makes 8 to 10 servings.

For a 5, 6 or 7-quart Crock-Pot® slow cooker, double all ingredients, except for the white sauce. Increase the White Sauce ingredients by half.

MARINATED CHINESE CHICKEN SALAD

Did you know that Chinese chicken salad is not Chinese at all, but a very American dish? The dressing for the salad is easy to make, but you can substitute your favorite store-bought Asian-style salad dressing to make this dish even simpler to prepare.

Marinade:
3 cloves garlic, minced
1 Tbs. fresh ginger, grated
1 tsp. dried red chile flakes
2 Tbs. honey
3 Tbs. soy sauce
2 Tbs. sesame oil
6 boneless, skinless chicken breasts

Dressing:
½ cup rice wine vinegar
1 clove garlic, minced
1 tsp. ginger, grated
1 Tbs. honey

Salad:
1 large head iceberg lettuce, shredded
2 medium carrots, julienned
½ cup roasted whole peanuts, chopped
¼ cup fresh cilantro, chopped
½ package maifun noodles, fried in hot oil

In a small mixing bowl, combine the marinade ingredients. Place the chicken in the Crock-Pot® slow cooker and pour the marinade over, making sure each chicken breast is well-coated. Cover; cook on Low 6 to 8 hours (High: 3 to 4 hours). Remove the chicken from the stoneware and cool. Shred into bite-sized pieces. In a small mixing bowl, combine the dressing ingredients with ½ cup of the juice from the slow cooker. In a large serving bowl, toss together the shredded chicken, lettuce, carrots, peanuts, cilantro and maifun noodles. Shortly before serving, drizzle with the salad dressing. Toss well and serve. Makes 6 to 8 servings.

For a 5, 6 or 7-quart Crock-Pot® slow cooker, double all ingredients.

BBQ TURKEY SMOKEY JOES

This recipe makes great open-faced sandwiches and you can round out the meal with french fries and fresh fruit salad.

3 lbs. ground turkey
1 onion, finely chopped
1 green pepper, seeded and finely chopped
2–8 oz. cans tomato sauce
¾ cup ketchup
¼ cup brown sugar
3 Tbs. cider vinegar

1 Tbs. liquid smoke
1 Tbs. Worcestershire sauce
1 tsp. cayenne pepper
¼ tsp. freshly ground black pepper
¼ tsp. garlic powder
10 onion sandwich rolls, split and toasted

For a 5, 6 or 7-quart Crock-Pot® slow cooker, double the ingredients except the ketchup, sugar and vinegar.

Brown the turkey in a skillet and drain off the fat. Place the turkey in the Crock-Pot® slow cooker and add the remaining ingredients. Stir thoroughly. Cover; cook on Low 8 to 10 hours (or on High for 3 to 4 hours). To serve, spoon the turkey and sauce over the rolls. Makes 10 servings.

TARRAGON TURKEY & PASTA

1½ to 2 lbs. turkey tenderloins
¼ cup dry white wine
½ cup celery, thinly sliced
¼ cup green onions, thinly sliced
4 Tbs. fresh tarragon, minced
1 tsp. salt
1 tsp. freshly ground black pepper

½ cup plain yogurt
1 Tbs. fresh Italian parsley, minced
1 Tbs. lemon juice
1½ Tbs. cornstarch
2 Tbs. water
4 cups pasta of your choice, cooked al denté

An easy dish that is elegant enough to serve at a dinner party.

Combine the turkey, wine, celery, green onions, 2 Tbs. fresh tarragon, salt and pepper in the Crock-Pot® slow cooker. Mix thoroughly. Cover; cook on Low 6 to 8 hours (or on High for 3½ to 4 hours). After cooking, remove the turkey from the stoneware and cut into ½-inch medallions. Turn the slow cooker to High. Add the yogurt, 2 Tbs. fresh tarragon, parsley and lemon juice to the juice in the stoneware. In a small bowl, combine the cornstarch and water. Pour over the juices to thicken the sauce. Once the sauce has thickened, serve the turkey medallions over the pasta, drizzled with the tarragon sauce from the slow cooker.

For a 5, 6 or 7-quart Crock-Pot® slow cooker, double all ingredients.

CRANBERRY-ORANGE TURKEY BREAST

The complementary flavors of cranberry and orange are combined to give this turkey breast some tangy zest.

½ cup orange marmalade
1–16 oz. can whole cranberries in sauce
2 tsp. orange zest, grated
3 lbs. turkey breast

For the 5, 6 or 7-quart Crock-Pot® slow cooker, double all ingredients.

In a medium bowl, combine the orange marmalade, cranberries, and orange zest. Place the turkey breast in the Crock-Pot® slow cooker and pour the orange-cranberry mixture over the turkey. Cover; cook on Low for 8 to 10 hours (or on High for 4 to 5 hours), or until the internal temperature of the turkey reaches 185°F. Makes 6 servings.

TURKEY MADEIRA TETRAZZINI

2 lbs. turkey breast tenders
½ cup chicken broth
¼ cup Madeira wine
2 oz. dried porcini mushrooms
1 medium onion, thinly sliced
½ cup heavy cream
1 cup asparagus, cut in 2-inch pieces, cooked until tender-crisp
¼ cup fresh Italian parsley, finely chopped
16 oz. spaghetti noodles, cooked al denté and drained

A rich sauce of wine, cream and mushrooms envelopes the turkey breast tenders and asparagus to create a delicious entrée.

Place the turkey in the Crock-Pot® slow cooker. In a medium bowl, combine the chicken broth, wine, mushrooms, and onion. Pour this mixture over the turkey. Cover; cook on low 6 to 8 hours (or on High for 3 to 4 hours). Remove the turkey from the stoneware and cut into bite-sized pieces. Add the heavy cream, asparagus and parsley to the slow cooker liquid and mix thoroughly to combine. Return the turkey to this sauce. Place the spaghetti noodles on a large serving platter and carefully pour the sauce over the noodles. Makes 8 servings.

For a 5, 6 or 7-quart Crock-Pot® slow cooker, double all ingredients.

TURKEY TAMALE PIE

An old family favorite, this dish uncovers flavors that are deep and satisfying. Serve with crusty sourdough rolls and a fresh green salad.

1 medium onion, chopped
1 clove garlic, minced
1 Tbs. vegetable oil
1 lb. ground turkey
1 tsp. freshly ground black pepper
¼ tsp. cayenne pepper
¼ tsp. salt

1 cup yellow cornmeal
1½ cups chicken broth
1 egg, beaten
1–14 oz. can of creamed corn
1–14 oz. can plum tomatoes, drained and chopped
1–14 oz. can black olives, drained

You may double all the ingredients when using the 5, 6 or 7-quart Crock-Pot® slow cooker.

In a medium skillet, sauté the onion and garlic in the oil. Add the ground turkey to brown. Season with the black pepper, cayenne pepper and salt. Drain any liquid from the skillet. In the Crock-Pot® slow cooker, combine the skillet contents, cornmeal, broth, egg, creamed corn, plum tomatoes, and olives. Mix thoroughly. Cover; cook on High for 1 hour, then on Low for 3 hours. Makes 6 servings.

FRESH HERBED TURKEY BREAST

⅛ cup butter, softened

¼ cup fresh sage, minced

¼ cup fresh tarragon, minced

2 cloves garlic, minced

1 tsp. freshly ground black pepper

½ tsp. salt

1–4 lb. turkey breast

1½ Tbs. cornstarch

Fresh herbs enliven this simple, excellent main dish.

In a small bowl, create a compound butter by mixing together the softened butter, sage, tarragon, garlic, pepper and salt. Rub this compound butter all over the turkey breast. Place the turkey breast in the Crock-Pot® slow cooker. Cover; cook on Low 8 to 10 hours (or on High for 4 to 5 hours). Remove the turkey breast from the stoneware. While the slow cooker is on High, slowly whisk in the cornstarch to thicken the sauce. When the sauce is thick and smooth, pour over the turkey breast. Slice to serve. Makes 8 servings.

For 5, 6 or 7-quart Crock-Pot® slow cooker, double all ingredients.

LEMON-GARLIC TURKEY BREAST

Perfect when served with spinach fettuccini and a salad of field greens!

1–3 lb. turkey breast
½ cup lemon juice
6 cloves garlic, minced
¼ tsp. dried parsley
¼ tsp. dried tarragon
¼ tsp. dried rosemary
¼ tsp. dried sage
¼ tsp. salt
¼ tsp. freshly ground black pepper
½ cup white wine

For a 5, 6 or 7-quart Crock-Pot® slow cooker, double all ingredients.

Place the turkey breast in the Crock-Pot® slow cooker. In a small bowl, combine the lemon juice, garlic, parsley, tarragon, rosemary, sage, salt, pepper and wine. Pour this sauce over the turkey breast. Cover; cook on Low 8 to 10 hours (or on High for 4 to 5 hours). Slice before serving. Makes 6 servings.

CHAPTER 5

FLAVORFUL CROCK-POT®
SLOW COOKER FISH &
SHELLFISH RECIPES

Seafood offers a wide variety of flavors–from the sweetness of prawns to the succulence of river salmon. Not only is it delicious, but nutritionists also promote the eating of seafood because it is low in cholesterol and fat and high in protein. In addition, some fish, such as mackerel and salmon, are high in omega-three fatty acids, a recommended supplement to the diet.

Many cooks are intimidated by cooking fish and shellfish because of the varied cooking times and unfamiliar preparatory steps. However, because slow-cooking in the Crock-Pot® slow cooker is one of the best ways to cook fish, shellfish stews and casseroles, you can be assured that our flavorful recipes will offer your family and friends the best of seafood cookery. Slow cooking truly extracts the sophisticated flavors of the bounty of the sea and blends them with the satisfying seasonings imparted by other fresh ingredients. And, as a nice bonus, these recipes are exceptionally easy to follow and clean-up is a breeze.

VALENCIAN SEAFOOD PAELLA

Fresh seafood provides a healthful complement to this traditional Spanish fare. And, saffron, which is a small, but key ingredient in paella, adds a golden color and subtle flavor to this delicious entrée.

You may double all the ingredients when using a 5, 6 or 7-quart Crock-Pot® slow cooker.

1 cup long grain white rice
2 cups water (you may substitute chicken broth, if desired)
1 small onion, diced
1 medium tomato, diced
pinch of ground saffron
3 cloves garlic, finely minced
¼ tsp. cayenne pepper
1 tsp. salt

1 tsp. freshly ground black pepper
½ lb. fresh mild fish fillets, cut into 1-inch pieces
½ lb. fresh sea scallops, cleaned
½ lb. fresh medium shrimp (uncooked), shelled and tails removed
8 oz. frozen peas, thawed and drained
1 lemon, cut in wedges

Place the rice, water, onion, tomato, saffron, garlic, cayenne pepper, salt and pepper in the Crock-Pot® slow cooker and mix thoroughly. Cook on High for 2 to 3 hours. Add the fish fillets, sea scallops, shrimp and peas to the paella and cook on High for 1 hour. Serve with lemon wedges as a garnish. Serves 4.

SAN FRANCISCO CIOPPINO

1–28 oz. can crushed tomatoes, undrained

1–8 oz. can tomato sauce

1 medium onion, chopped

1 cup white wine

1 cup water

¼ cup olive oil

½ cup fresh Italian parsley, chopped

4 cloves garlic, minced

2 tsp. dried sweet basil

1 tsp. dried thyme

1 tsp. dried oregano

½ tsp. red pepper flakes

½ tsp. cayenne pepper

½ lb. fresh or frozen cod or other whitefish fillets, thawed and cut into bite-sized pieces

½ lb. fresh prawns, peeled and deveined

⅓ lb. fresh scallops

½ lb. fresh mussels

½ lb. fresh clams

2 lemons, cut into wedges

This San Francisco classic is best served with sourdough bread or fragrant garlic bread. Be sure to have a bowl on the side in which to discard the shells of the mussels and clams.

Combine all ingredients, except the seafood and lemons, in the Crock-Pot® slow cooker. Cover; cook on Low 6 to 8 hours (or on High for 3 to 4 hours). Thirty minutes before serving, add the seafood to the stoneware and turn to High. To serve, squeeze lemon wedges into each serving. Makes 6 servings.

You may double all the ingredients when using a 5, 6 or 7-quart Crock-Pot® slow cooker.

SHRIMP JAMBALAYA

This traditional Cajun dish has a delectable combination of different meats and shrimp, with a kick of spice. You can add more hot sauce and cayenne pepper to reach your optimum level of spiciness.

For a 5, 6 or 7-quart Crock-Pot® slow cooker, double all ingredients.

12 oz. boneless, skinless chicken breasts
8 oz. smoked sausage of your choice
8 oz. smoked ham, diced
1 green pepper, finely chopped
1 medium onion, chopped
2 stalks celery, finely sliced
4 cloves garlic, minced
1–14½ oz. can whole tomatoes
⅓ cup tomato paste

1 cup chicken broth
1 Tbs. dried parsley
1½ tsp. dried basil leaves
½ tsp. dried oregano leaves
1½ tsp. prepared hot sauce
1½ tsp. cayenne pepper
1 tsp. black pepper
salt to taste
1 lb. fresh shrimp, shelled and cleaned
4 cups cooked rice

Cut the chicken into bite-sized pieces. Add all remaining ingredients, except the shrimp and rice, to the Crock-Pot® slow cooker. Cover; cook on Low 8 to 10 hours (or on High for 3 to 4 hours). Add the shrimp during the last 30 minutes of cooking. Pour the Shrimp Jambalaya over the rice when ready to serve. Makes 6 servings.

CREAMY NEW ENGLAND CLAM CHOWDER

3 slices bacon, diced
1 medium onion, chopped
2–8 oz. cans clams, drained
3 cloves garlic, minced
3 medium potatoes, pared and cubed
1½ cups water
1 tsp. salt
½ tsp. pepper
1–13 oz. can evaporated milk

This simple soup is hard to resist! The classic combination of clams, bacon and potatoes in a creamy, warm soup will leave a delicious impression on your family and guests.

In a small skillet, sauté the bacon and onion until golden. Drain and put into the Crock-Pot® slow cooker. Add all remaining ingredients, except the evaporated milk. Cover; cook on Low 6 to 9 hours (or on High for 2 to 4 hours) or until the potatoes are tender. Add the evaporated milk during last hour of cooking and blend well. Makes 4 servings.

For a 5, 6 or 7-quart Crock-Pot® slow cooker, double all ingredients.

SALMON & PARMESAN RICE CASSEROLE

Perfect for a cold winter evening! These rich and satisfying flavors will chase away any chill.

2 cups long-grained converted
    white rice, uncooked
1–16 oz. can salmon, drained and
    flaked
1 cup cauliflower florets
1 cup Parmesan cheese, grated
1 cup dry white wine
1 cup milk

1 cup water
1 Tbs. fresh tarragon, minced
1 tsp. Dijon mustard
1½ tsp. salt
½ tsp. freshly ground black pepper
1 cup fresh tomatoes, diced
½ cup green onions, thinly sliced

For a 5, 6 or 7-
quart Crock-Pot®
slow cooker,
double all
ingredients.

Combine all ingredients, except for the tomatoes and green onions, in the Crock-Pot® slow cooker. Mix thoroughly. Cover; cook on High for one hour, then on Low 6 to 8 hours (or on High for 3 to 4 hours). Before serving, stir in the tomatoes and green onions. Makes 6 servings.

ASIAN SWEET & SOUR SHRIMP

1–13 oz. can of pineapple, drained (reserve ½ cup of the juice)

2 celery stalks, sliced

2 medium tomatoes, cut into small wedges

1 cup broccoli florets

1 medium onion, chopped

1 cup chicken broth

3 cloves garlic, minced

3 Tbs. sugar

1 Tbs. white vinegar

2 tsp. fish sauce (optional)

2 tsp. soy sauce

½ tsp. fresh ginger, minced

½ lb. medium shrimp, peeled and deveined

2 Tbs. cornstarch

⅓ cup water

The tartness of this dish is countered by the sweetness of the pineapple. Serve over white rice for a complete meal.

Combine all ingredients in Crock-Pot® slow cooker, except for the shrimp, cornstarch and water. Cover; cook on Low 4 to 6 hours (or on High for 2 to 3 hours). During the final 30 minutes of cooking, add the shrimp to the stoneware. Set the slow cooker to High. Whisk together the cornstarch and water and add to the sauce in the stoneware. Stir to blend and thicken. Makes 6 servings.

For a 5, 6 or 7-quart Crock-Pot® slow cooker: double all ingredients, except for the chicken broth.

HALIBUT STEAKS IN A LEMONY WINE SAUCE

Halibut is a firm white fish that deserves the bright flavors of lemon and wine. Serve with seasonal vegetables and pasta.

2 packages (12 oz. each) frozen or fresh halibut steaks (or any other firm white fish)
¼ cup butter
2 Tbs. flour
⅓ cup dry white wine
⅓ cup heavy cream

½ tsp. salt
½ tsp. freshly ground black pepper
¼ cup fresh lemon juice
1 tsp. lemon zest, grated
1 Tbs. fresh sage, minced
1 Tbs. fresh Italian parsley, minced

For a 5, 6 or 7-quart Crock-Pot® slow cooker, you may double all the ingredients.

Pat halibut steaks dry and place in the Crock-Pot® slow cooker. In a medium saucepan, melt the butter and slowly whisk in the flour to create a roux. When slightly browned, add the wine and cream, constantly whisking over medium heat until the sauce has thickened. Add the salt, pepper, lemon juice, and lemon zest. Pour the sauce over the fish. Cover; cook on High 2½ to 3 hours. Shortly before serving, add the fresh sage and parsley to the sauce and mix until well combined. Makes 6 servings.

CLAMS FLORENTINE

2–6½ oz. cans chopped clams, drained
1–10 oz. package frozen chopped spinach, thawed and well-drained
½ cup Parmesan cheese, grated
½ cup bread crumbs
⅓ cup onion, chopped
¼ cup unsalted butter or margarine, melted
1½ cups half-and-half
½ tsp. salt
½ tsp. freshly ground black pepper
1 lb. egg noodles, cooked al denté and drained

This creamy casserole combines the ocean-flavor of clams with the freshness of spinach and aged Parmesan cheese.

Lightly grease the Crock-Pot® slow cooker. Combine all ingredients in the stoneware, except the noodles, and mix thoroughly. Cover; cook on Low 4 to 6 hours (or on High for 2 to 3 hours). To serve, prepare individual plates with the noodles and spoon the clams and sauce over the noodles. Makes 8 servings.

You may double all the ingredients when using a 5, 6 or 7-quart Crock-Pot® slow cooker.

CHAPTER 6

FAVORITE CROCK-POT®
SLOW COOKER RECIPES
FROM AROUND THE WORLD

The Crock-Pot® slow cooker is the perfect place to experiment with new and exciting cuisines. Like traditional American slow cooker favorites, there are plenty of recipes from other cultures that translate easily into slow-cooking. Ethnic cooking is a growing trend and understandably so; the dishes are succulent, savory and offer new culinary experiences for all of us.

This chapter contains recipes from all around the world: Mexico, Japan, India, Italy, Thailand, Indonesia, France and Cuba. Amazingly, these international dishes do not require exotic ingredients, but their uniqueness is found in the unusual combinations of basic ingredients. We've made sure that the ingredients for these dishes are easily found in your local supermarket. All of these recipes are perfect for your slow cooker: limited preparatory steps, simple combinations and easy clean-up. Best of all, you can surprise your family or guests with an authentic ethnic meal, from Indian Lamb Korma with Cucumber Raita to Japanese Kinpura Gobo. So, enjoy!

COZUMEL TORTILLA SOUP

This slightly spicy soup is a Mexican classic. Serve as a first course or a beautiful vegetarian entrée.

4 cloves garlic, minced
1 medium onion, chopped
1 tsp. prepared hot sauce
2 jalapeño peppers, seeded and minced
2–8 oz. cans tomato sauce
4 cups chicken broth
2 limes, cut into wedges
1 ripe avocado, cut into bite-sized pieces
6 oz. crumbly fresh cheese, such as feta
tortilla chips, crumbled, for garnish

For a 5, 6 or 7-quart Crock-Pot® slow cooker, double all ingredients.

Combine the garlic, onion, hot sauce, peppers, tomato sauce and chicken broth in the Crock-Pot® slow cooker. Cover; Cook on Low 4 to 6 hours (or on High for 2 to 3 hours). Ladle the soup into serving bowls and squeeze lime wedges into each bowl. Top with the fresh avocado, cheese, and crumbled tortilla chips. Makes 6 servings.

INDONESIAN BEEF RENDANG

2 medium onions, roughly
  chopped
3 cloves garlic, roughly chopped
1 Tbs. fresh ginger, chopped
4 small red chile peppers, seeded
  and chopped
½ cup water

2 lbs. round steak, cut into
  1½-inch cubes
2 tsp. ground coriander
2 tbs. tamarind sauce
1 tsp. ground turmeric
2 tsp. curry powder
stem of lemon grass, 4 inches long
2 cups coconut milk

*Serve this with
fragrant jasmine rice.*

In a food processor, blend onions, garlic, ginger, chili peppers, and water until smooth. Add this mixture, the steak, and the rest of the ingredients to the Crock-Pot® slow cooker, and combine thoroughly. Cover; cook on Low 8 to 10 hours (or on High for 4 to 6 hours). Halfway through cooking, remove the lid and mix thoroughly to prevent the coconut milk from separating. Replace the cover. Remove the lemon grass before serving. Makes 6 servings.

For a 5, 6 or 7-quart Crock-Pot® slow cooker, double all ingredients, except for the water and coconut milk.

SOUTHEAST ASIAN SEAFOOD STEW

The tangy broth of this seafood stew has a fresh, clean taste. Served with white rice, this stew is especially satisfying.

1–8 oz. can tomato sauce

1 medium onion, chopped

1 cup white wine

1 cup chicken or vegetable stock

¼ cup vegetable oil

¼ cup fresh lime juice

½ cup fresh coriander or cilantro, chopped

3 medium tomatoes, cut into small wedges

4 cloves garlic, minced

2 tsp. ginger, grated

½ tsp. red pepper flakes

½ tsp. cayenne pepper

½ lb. fresh or frozen cod or other whitefish fillets, thawed and cut into bite-sized pieces

⅓ lb. fresh prawns, peeled and deveined

⅓ lb. fresh scallops

½ lb. fresh mussels or clams

cilantro sprigs, for garnish

2 limes, cut into wedges

Combine all ingredients in the Crock-Pot® slow cooker, except for shellfish, limes and cilantro sprigs. Cover; cook on Low 6 to 8 hours (or on High for 3 to 4 hours). Thirty minutes before serving, add the shellfish to the stoneware and turn the temperature to High. Garnish with cilantro sprigs and serve with lime wedges. Makes 6 servings.

For 5, 6 or 7-quart Crock-Pot® slow cooker, double all ingredients, except for the tomato sauce, white wine, chicken stock, vegetable oil and lime juice.

CHEESE & CHILE ENCHILADA CASSEROLE

Out-of-this-world spicy seasonings meet beef, cheese and all the Mexican fixings for a perfect partnership!

1 large onion, diced
2 cloves garlic, minced
1 Tbs. vegetable oil
2 lbs. ground beef
1 pkg. taco seasoning mix
1 cup cream of mushroom soup
1–4 oz. can of diced green chilies
12 corn tortillas
1 cup Jack cheese, shredded
1 cup cheddar cheese, shredded
1 cup sour cream
1 cup tomatillo salsa
1–4 oz. can of sliced black olives
1/4 cup green onions, sliced thinly

In a medium skillet, sauté the onion and garlic in the oil. Add the ground beef to brown. Drain the fat from the beef. Add the taco seasoning and mix thoroughly. In a mixing bowl, combine the cream of mushroom soup with the diced green chilies. In the Crock-Pot® slow cooker, spoon in 3 Tbs. of the soup mixture and spread to cover the bottom of the stoneware. Create the next layer with 3 tortillas, ¼ cup of the soup mixture, ⅓ of the ground beef mixture, ½ cup of a combination of the cheeses. Continue making these layers until you use all the ingredients. Cover; cook on Low 6 to 8 hours (or on High for 3 to 4 hours). In a small mixing bowl, combine the sour cream and tomatillo salsa. Top each serving with the sour cream salsa, a sprinkling of black olives, and a garnish of green onions. Makes 6 servings.

For a 5, 6 or 7-quart Crock-Pot® slow cooker, double all ingredients.

INDONESIAN COCONUT CHICKEN

Serve with Fruit Skewers with Apricot Ginger Dipping Sauce *(p. 34) for an exotic meal.*

2 cloves garlic, minced
½ tsp. salt
½ tsp. freshly ground black pepper
2 tsp. ground cumin
2 tsp. ground coriander
½ tsp. ground fennel
½ tsp. ground cinnamon

2 lbs. chicken drumsticks
2 medium onions, finely sliced
1 cup coconut milk
1 cup water
1 Tbs. lemon juice
¼ cup scallions, sliced, for garnish

For a 5, 6 or 7-quart Crock-Pot® slow cooker, double all ingredients, except for the water.

In a small bowl, combine the garlic, salt, pepper, cumin, coriander, fennel, and cinnamon. Rub the mixture all over the chicken drumsticks. Place the chicken, any leftover seasoning mixture, onions, coconut milk, water and lemon juice in the Crock-Pot® slow cooker. Cover; cook on Low 6 to 8 hours (or on High for 3 to 4 hours). Garnish with scallions.

MILANO MINESTRONE SOUP

1 cup smoked ham, diced
1 medium onion, finely chopped
2 cloves garlic, minced
2 medium carrots, diced
2 celery stalks, diced
2 zucchini, diced
1 medium potato, diced
1 cup green cabbage, shredded
1–14½ oz. can of crushed tomatoes, drained

1–15 oz. can kidney beans, drained and rinsed
4 cups vegetable broth
2 Tbs. dried parsley
1 Tbs. dried sweet basil
½ cup elbow macaroni, cooked al denté and drained
salt to taste

This substantial Italian classic is a great way to eat your vegetables. Serve with crusty French bread and a green salad for a complete and satisfying meal.

Combine all ingredients, except for the macaroni, in the Crock-Pot® slow cooker. Mix thoroughly. Cover; cook on Low 8–9 hours (or on High for 3–4 hours). Add the macaroni during the last hour of cooking. Add salt to taste. Serves 6.

You may double all ingredients when using a 5, 6 or 7-quart Crock-Pot® slow cooker.

BANGKOK STEAK SALAD

This succulent steak salad is best made in the height of summer, when fresh mint, cilantro and basil are at their most fragrant. The slightly sweet peanut vinaigrette is a delicious counterpoint to the robustly flavored flank steak.

2 Tbs. soy sauce
2 Tbs. vegetable oil
4 cloves garlic, minced
1 Tbs. ginger, grated
1 Tbs. lemon grass, finely sliced (or 1 Tbs. lemon juice)
1 Tbs. Asian fish sauce
1 tsp. Asian chile paste
1½ lb. beef flank steak, trimmed of excess fat

Vinaigrette:
2 Tbs. creamy peanut butter
2 Tbs. rice wine vinegar
1 Tbs. fresh lime juice
salt and pepper to taste
1 green cabbage, thinly shredded (or equivalent coleslaw mix)
2 medium carrots, thinly julienned
½ cup fresh mint, coarsely chopped
½ cup fresh cilantro, coarsely chopped
½ cup fresh basil, coarsely chopped
¼ cup green onions, finely sliced
¼ cup unsalted peanuts, toasted and coarsely chopped

In a small mixing bowl, whisk together the soy sauce, vegetable oil, garlic, ginger, lemon grass (or lemon juice), fish sauce, and chile paste. Place the flank steak in the Crock-Pot® slow cooker and pour the sauce over the steak, making sure to coat the steak well. Cover and cook on Low 6 to 8 hours (or on High for 3 to 4 hours). Remove the flank steak and reserve ½ cup of the liquid in the slow cooker. Let the steak stand 10 minutes before slicing thinly across the grain of the meat.

Assemble the salad vinaigrette by whisking together the reserved stoneware liquid, peanut butter, rice wine vinegar and lime juice. Add salt and pepper to taste. In a large mixing bowl, combine the green cabbage, carrots, mint, cilantro, basil and green onions. Dress with the salad vinaigrette and toss well. Divide the salad onto individual plates, and place slices of steak across each plate. Garnish with a sprinkling of the chopped peanuts. Makes 6 servings.

For a 5, 6 or 7-quart Crock-Pot® slow cooker, you may double all ingredients.

INDIAN LAMB KORMA

This traditional Indian dish is a flavorful option for lamb. Serve with basmathi rice and a side of Cucumber Raita *(p. 111) for an exotic, yet simple meal.*

For a 5, 6 or 7-quart Crock-Pot® slow cooker, double all ingredients, except for the water and heavy cream.

2 large onions, chopped
2 tsp. ginger, finely grated
3 cloves garlic, minced
2 large dried chile peppers, seeded and de-stemmed, finely minced
2 Tbs. vegetable oil
¾ tsp. ground turmeric
2 tsp. ground cumin
1 Tbs. ground coriander

1½ lb. boneless lamb, cut into 1-inch cubes
⅔ cup ripe tomatoes, chopped
¼ tsp. ground cloves
½ tsp. ground cinnamon
¼ tsp. ground cardamom
¼ tsp. freshly ground black pepper
½ cup water
½ cup heavy cream.

In a medium skillet, sauté the onion, ginger, garlic and chilies in the vegetable oil. Add the turmeric, cumin and coriander to further flavor the vegetable oil. Add the lamb to brown. Once the lamb has browned, pour the skillet contents into the Crock-Pot® slow cooker. Add the tomatoes, ground cloves, ground cinnamon, ground cardamom, black pepper and water and mix thoroughly. Cover; cook on Low 6 to 8 hours (or on High for 3 to 4 hours). Thirty minutes before serving, stir in the heavy cream and re-cover. Makes 6 servings.

CUCUMBER RAITA

1 large cucumber, seeded and grated
1 tsp. salt
½ cup plain yogurt
2 Tbs. fresh mint, chopped

A cool and refreshing sauce!

In a small bowl, sprinkle cucumber with salt, and let stand for 5 minutes. Drain off the cucumber liquid. Stir in yogurt and mint, and serve with the Indian Lamb Korma.

All ingredients may be doubled or even tripled when serving as an accompaniment to large entrées.

SALSA STEAK FAJITAS

This flavorful dish is an easy dinner when served with store-bought tortillas, rice and beans.

½ cup salsa of your choice (fire-roasted salsa works best)
1 clove garlic, minced
1 Tbs. fresh lime juice
1 tsp. freshly ground black pepper
½ tsp. salt
1½ lbs. beef flank steak, trimmed of excess fat
1 red bell pepper, cut into ¼-inch strips
1 yellow bell pepper, cut into ¼-inch strips
1 green bell pepper, cut into ¼-inch strips
1 large onion, thinly sliced
2 tsp. fresh cilantro, minced, for garnish

For a 5, 6 or 7-quart Crock-Pot® slow cooker, double all ingredients, except for the salsa.

In a small mixing bowl, combine the salsa, garlic, lime juice, salt and pepper. Place the flank steak in the Crock-Pot® slow cooker and pour the sauce over the steak, making sure to coat the steak well. Add the bell peppers and onion to the stoneware. Cover and cook on Low 6 to 8 hours (or on High for 3 to 4 hours). Remove the flank steak and vegetables from the juice and let the steak stand 10 minutes before slicing. Slice the steak thinly across the grain of the meat. Serve with the peppers and onion. Garnish with the fresh cilantro. Makes 6 servings.

HEARTY BLACK BEAN SOUP

1 lb. black beans, soaked overnight and drained
2 Tbs. vegetable oil
1 large onion, finely chopped
2 cloves garlic, minced
2 Tbs. fresh cilantro or Italian parsley, minced
2 quarts chicken or vegetable stock
¼ cup crumbly fresh cheese, such as feta cheese

This rich soup has an earthy sweetness that is hard to resist. Serve with tortilla chips and lime wedges for an extra dimension.

Combine all ingredients, except the cheese, in the Crock-Pot® slow cooker. Cover; cook on High 2 hours, then on Low 8-10 hours. To assemble, sprinkle the cheese evenly in eight individual bowls and pour the soup over the cheese. Makes 8 servings.

For a 5, 6 or 7-quart Crock-Pot® slow cooker, double all ingredients, except for the chicken stock.

NIKU JAGA

This Japanese beef stew is a delicious one pot meal. Serve with sticky white rice on the side.

2 lbs. beef stew meat, cut in 1-inch cubes
1 cup water
½ cup Japanese sake (or dry white wine)
¼ cup sugar
¼ cup soy sauce
1 tsp. salt
4 medium carrots, sliced on the bias
3 medium potatoes, peeled and chopped
1 white onion, chopped

For a 5, 6 or 7-quart Crock-Pot® slow cooker, increase all ingredients, except for the water, sake, sugar and soy sauce.

Combine all the ingredients in the Crock-Pot® slow cooker. Cover; cook on Low 10 to 12 hours (or on High for 4 to 6 hours). Stir stew thoroughly before serving. Makes 6 servings.

FRENCH ONION SOUP

4 large onions, diced
½ cup butter
2 Tbs. flour
6 cups beef stock
1 tsp. salt
6 thick slices of baguette, toasted
1 cup mozzarella cheese, shredded
1 Tbs. fresh chives, finely chopped, as garnish

The cheese and bread toppings accent the subtle, buttery flavor of this soup and the garnish of chives gives it a splash of color.

In a large skillet, sauté the onions in the butter. Add the flour and mix thoroughly. Add the onion mixture to the Crock-Pot® slow cooker. Add the beef stock and salt. Cover; cook on Low 8 to 10 hours (or on High for 4-5 hours). Ladle the soup into ovenproof bowls and top with the bread and cheese. Broil in the oven until the cheese is melted. Sprinkle with fresh chives. Makes 6 servings.

You may double all the ingredients when using a 5, 6 or 7-quart Crock-Pot® slow cooker.

THAI GREEN CURRY

Serve with steamed jasmine rice for a completely delectable meal.

1 cup unsweetened coconut milk

2 Tbs. green curry paste

1 stalk lemon grass, cut into 1-inch pieces

1 cup chicken broth

2 Tbs. fish sauce

2 Tbs. sugar

2 cloves garlic, minced

1 tsp. fresh ginger, grated

½ tsp. ground turmeric

2 Tbs. fresh lime juice

1½ lb. boneless, skinless chicken breast, sliced into strips

½ cup frozen peas

2 Tbs. fresh cilantro, minced

For a 5, 6 or 7-quart Crock-Pot® slow cooker, double all ingredients.

In a small mixing bowl, whisk together the coconut milk and curry paste. In the Crock-Pot® slow cooker, add this mixture and combine all the remaining ingredients, except for the frozen peas and cilantro. Mix thoroughly. Cover; cook on Low 6 to 8 hours (or on High for 3 to 4 hours). During the last 15 minutes of cooking, add the frozen peas and cilantro. Remove the lemon grass from the curry before serving. Makes 6 servings.

VICHYSSOISE

2 large leeks, chopped
2 medium potatoes, peeled and chopped
3 cups chicken stock
2 Tbs. chives, chopped
1 cup milk
½ cup heavy cream
grated nutmeg, for garnish

Traditionally, this smooth and creamy soup is served chilled, but it is equally delicious when served warm. It is a beautiful first course for an elegant meal.

Combine the leeks, potatoes, chicken stock and chives in the Crock-Pot® slow cooker. Cover; cook on Low 4 to 6 hours (or on High for 2 to 3 hours). After cooking, add the milk and allow the soup to cool. Place the soup in a food processor or blender. Puree for 1 minute or until smooth. Transfer to a large bowl and add cream. Stir thoroughly. Serve sprinkled with nutmeg. Makes 6 servings.

For a 5, 6 or 7-quart Crock-Pot® slow cooker, you may double all ingredients.

ARROZ CON POLLO

Many Latin American countries have their own version of this traditional Spanish dish. This main entrée owes its vibrant yellow color to the saffron.

pinch of saffron
2 Tbs. boiling water
1 Tbs. vegetable oil
1 large onion, chopped
2 cloves garlic, minced
1 green bell pepper, seeded and chopped
1 cup converted, long-grain rice
2 bay leaves
1 tsp. dried oregano
½ tsp. paprika
1 tsp. salt
½ tsp. freshly ground pepper
1–14 oz. can plum tomatoes, drained and chopped
8 boneless chicken thighs
salt and pepper to taste
1½ cups lowfat, low-sodium chicken broth
1 cup frozen peas, defrosted

In a small bowl, combine the saffron and boiling water and set aside. In a large skillet, sauté the onion, garlic, pepper and rice in the vegetable oil. Season with the bay leaves, oregano, paprika, salt and pepper. Add the plum tomatoes and place in the bottom of the Crock-Pot® slow cooker. Season the chicken thighs with salt and pepper. In the same skillet, sauté the chicken thighs until browned. Place the chicken thighs on top of the rice layer in the stoneware. Add the saffron and water, and the chicken broth. Cover; cook on High for 1 hour, then reduce heat to Low for 7 to 9 hours. Thirty minutes before the end of cooking, add the frozen peas to the slow cooker and mix the contents thoroughly. Makes 4 servings.

For a 5, 6 or 7-quart Crock-Pot® slow cooker, you may double all ingredients.

KINPURA GOBO

Kinpura Gobo combines the nutritional benefits of burdock root (known in Japan as "gobo") with sweet and salty flavors imparted by the soy sauce and sugar. You can find burdock root in the produce section of your grocery store or in specialty Asian markets. Serve over steaming bowls of sticky white rice.

1 lb. ground beef
2 medium burdock roots, peeled and julienned
2 medium carrots, peeled and julienned
1–14 oz. can black beans, rinsed and drained
2 Tbs. sesame oil
¼ cup sake or dry white wine
3 Tbs. sugar
¼ cup soy sauce
2 cups water

For a 5, 6 or 7-quart Crock-Pot® slow cooker, double all ingredients.

In a medium skillet, brown the ground beef and drain off any excess fat. Transfer the ground beef to the Crock-Pot® slow cooker and add the remaining ingredients, mixing thoroughly. Cover; cook on Low 8 to 10 hours (or on High for 4 to 5 hours). Makes 4 servings.

MOROS

2 Tbs. olive oil
1 medium onion, chopped
2 cloves garlic, minced
1 green bell pepper, seeded and chopped
2 medium tomatoes, chopped
1–15 oz. can black beans, drained
1 cup long grain, converted rice
2 cups water or chicken stock

This lively and delicious side dish is a typical accompaniment to any Cuban meal.

In a medium skillet, sauté the onion, garlic and bell pepper in the olive oil until soft. Transfer the vegetables and oil to the Crock-Pot® slow cooker and add the remaining ingredients, mixing until thoroughly combined. Cover; cook on High for 1 hour, then reduce heat to Low for 7 to 9 hours. Makes 6 side servings.

You may double all the ingredients when using a 5, 6 or 7-quart Crock-Pot® slow cooker.

ROPA VIEJA

Serve warm flour tortillas with this spicy, flavorful Mexican stew to scoop up the meat, vegetables and pan juices. Delicious!

1½ lbs. flank steak, trimmed of excess fat
2 large carrots, cut into 1-inch slices
1 cup vegetable stock
1 large onion, diced
2 cloves garlic, minced
1 green bell pepper, seeded and chopped
½ tsp. cayenne pepper
1 tsp. salt
1 tsp. freshly ground black pepper
2 large tomatoes, chopped
2 jalapeños, seeded and minced
2 Tbs. tomato paste

Place the flank steak, carrots and vegetable stock in the Crock-Pot® slow cooker. Cover; cook on Low 7 to 9 hours (or on High for 3½ to 4½ hours). Remove the flank steak and carrot from the stoneware and shred the steak. Set aside. Reserve 1½ cups of the liquid from the stoneware. In a large pan, sauté the onion, garlic, and green pepper, seasoned with the cayenne pepper, salt, and black pepper, until soft. Add the tomatoes, jalapeños, and tomato paste to the pan, plus the 1½ cups of the reserved cooking juices. Bring to a boil and lower to a simmer, covered, for 20 minutes. During the last 5 minutes of simmering, uncover the pan and let the sauce reduce. Pour the sauce over individual servings of the carrots and shredded beef. Makes 4 servings.

For a 5, 6 or 7-quart Crock-Pot® slow cooker, double all ingredients.

CHAPTER 7

FAST & EASY CROCK-POT® SLOW COOKER MEALS FOR BUSY COOKS

If you are a busy cook, you will have even more reason to love your Crock-Pot® slow cooker! With a minimum of effort in the morning or even the night before, you can produce flavorful, family-friendly meals that everyone can enjoy. Imagine coming home from a hard day at work to the amazing aromas of a hot meal cooking in your slow cooker. Instead of eyeing a refrigerator and trying to decide what to make for dinner, you will revel in the knowledge that your slow cooker is doing the hard work for you. And, rather than relying on unhealthy fast-food, you will be providing your family with a home-cooked meal that is both delicious and soul-satisfying.

In this chapter, we have included recipes that are especially kid-friendly, from Barbecued Pulled Pork Sandwiches and Easy Family-Style Tacos to Mom's Best Macaroni & Cheese Dinner and Islander Chicken Drumsticks. Like our other dishes, these recipes are easy to prepare and simple to serve and clean-up. Sit back, enjoy your dinner and wait for the compliments from family and friends!

CORN AND CHEESE CHOWDER

This creamy soup is an excellent centerpiece for a delicious family dinner. Just serve the chowder with crusty French bread and a tossed green salad, and the meal is complete.

For a 5, 6 or 7-quart Crock-Pot® slow cooker, double all ingredients, except for the evaporated milk. Increase the evaporated milk to 19 oz.

1 large onion, finely chopped
1 clove garlic, minced
1 Tbs. vegetable oil
2 tsp. cumin seed
3 cups chicken stock
2 medium potatoes, peeled and chopped
1 cup canned creamed corn

2 cups fresh or frozen corn kernels
¼ cup fresh Italian parsley, chopped
1 cup cheddar cheese, grated
1-13 oz. can evaporated milk
2 Tbs. fresh chives, chopped

In a small skillet, sauté the onion and garlic in the oil until golden. Drain and put in the Crock-Pot® slow cooker. Add the remaining ingredients, except for the cheddar cheese, evaporated milk and chives. Mix thoroughly. Cover; cook on Low 6 to 9 hours or until the potatoes are tender (or on High for 2 to 4 hours). Add the cheese and evaporated milk during last hour of cooking and garnish with chives before serving. Makes 6 servings.

EASY FAMILY-STYLE TACOS

2 lbs. ground beef

1 medium onion, chopped

1–15 oz. can whole black or pinto beans

1 cup fresh or frozen kernel corn

1 can tomato sauce

1–4 oz. can diced green chilies

½ tsp. salt

¼ tsp. garlic powder

⅛ tsp. cayenne pepper (optional)

12 hard taco shells

½ cup tomatoes, diced

¼ head of iceberg lettuce, shredded

1½ cups cheddar cheese, grated

½ cup sour cream

Kids absolutely love tacos and parents will love this easy-to-make version. If you prefer, you may also substitute ground turkey for the ground beef.

In a large skillet, brown the onion and ground beef. Drain. Transfer to the Crock-Pot® slow cooker and add the beans, corn, tomato sauce, green chilies, salt, garlic powder, and cayenne pepper. Mix thoroughly. Cover; cook on Low 6 to 8 hours (or on High for 3 to 4 hours). Place the taco shells in a casserole dish, tightly packed so that they do not fall over. Spoon 3 tablespoons of the meat mixture into each taco shell, then a layer of tomato and lettuce, and a layer of cheese. Serve the tacos immediately with a dollop of sour cream on top of each, or place the tacos under a broiler to melt the cheese, then garnish each with sour cream. Makes 4 to 6 servings.

For a 5, 6 or 7-quart Crock-Pot® slow cooker, double all ingredients.

MOM'S BEST MACARONI & CHEESE DINNER

A childhood favorite is transformed into a main entrée for a family on the go.

For a 5, 6 or 7-quart Crock-Pot® slow cooker, double all ingredients, except for the milk. Increase the milk to ¾ cup.

1 medium onion, chopped
1 clove garlic, minced
3 Tbs. water
1–14 oz. can stewed tomatoes, drained and chopped
1 tsp. Italian seasoning
1 tsp. salt
¼ tsp. freshly ground black pepper
1½ cups cheddar cheese, grated
8 oz. macaroni pasta, cooked al denté and drained
½ cup milk
2 Tbs. butter or margarine, melted

In a medium skillet, brown the onion and garlic. Transfer the contents of the skillet to the Crock-Pot® slow cooker and add the water, tomatoes, Italian seasoning, salt and pepper. Mix thoroughly. Cover; cook on Low 6 to 8 hours (or on High for 3 to 4 hours). Thirty minutes before the end of the cooking time, add the cheddar cheese, macaroni, milk and butter. Mix thoroughly. Makes 4 servings.

CLASSIC ITALIAN BEEF SPAGHETTI

1 medium onion, chopped

2 cloves garlic, minced

1 green bell pepper, seeded and diced

1 stalk celery, sliced

1½ lbs. ground beef

1 medium carrot, diced

6 mushrooms, sliced

2–8 oz. cans tomato sauce

1½ cups water

1–14 oz. can stewed tomatoes, chopped, including the liquid

2 tsp. fresh oregano, minced

1 tsp. Italian parsley, minced

1½ tsp. salt

1 tsp. freshly ground black pepper

2 tsp. granulated sugar

8 oz. dry spaghetti, broken into thirds

A hearty meal best served with a sprinkling of freshly grated Parmesan cheese and a basket full of garlic bread.

In a medium skillet, sauté the onion, garlic, green pepper and celery. Brown the beef and drain. Add the skillet contents to the Crock-Pot® slow cooker. Add the carrot, mushrooms, tomato sauce, water, stewed tomatoes with the liquid, oregano, parsley, salt, pepper and sugar. Cover; cook on Low 6 to 8 hours (or on High for 3 to 5 hours). Turn to High during the last hour of cooking and stir in the dry spaghetti. Makes 6 servings.

You may double all the ingredients when using a 5, 6 or 7-quart Crock-Pot® slow cooker.

BARBECUED PULLED PORK SANDWICHES

This kid-popular dish is sweet and savory, and most importantly, extremely easy to make. Serve with crunchy coleslaw on the side.

2½ lbs. pork roast
1–14 oz. bottle of your favorite barbecue sauce
1 tsp. brown sugar
1 Tbs. fresh lemon juice
1 medium onion, chopped
8 hamburger buns or hard rolls

For a 5, 6 or 7-quart Crock-Pot® slow cooker, double all ingredients, except for the barbecue sauce. Increase the barbecue sauce to 21 oz.

Place the pork roast in Crock-Pot® slow cooker. Cover; cook on Low 10 to 12 hours (or on High for 5 to 6 hours). Remove the pork roast from the stoneware, and pull the meat into shredded pieces. Pour out any liquid in the stoneware, and combine the pork with the remaining ingredients in the slow cooker. Cook on High for 2 hours. Serve the barbecue pork on hamburger buns or hard rolls. Makes 8 servings.

SMOKED SAUSAGE WITH CABBAGE AND APPLES

1½ lbs. smoked sausage of your choice, cut into 2-inch lengths
3 cooking apples, thickly sliced
½ head of red cabbage, shredded
1 medium onion, sliced
½ cup brown sugar
1 tsp. salt
½ tsp. freshly ground black pepper
½ cup apple juice

Layer the sausage, apples, cabbage and onion in the Crock-Pot® slow cooker in the order listed above. Sprinkle the brown sugar, salt, and black pepper on top. Pour the apple juice over all the other ingredients. Do not stir. Cover; cook on Low 6 to 8 hours (or on High for 3 to 4 hours). Makes 6 servings.

Slow cooking allows the smooth, hearty flavors of sausage, cabbage and apples to perfectly blend.

For a 5, 6 or 7-quart Crock-Pot® slow cooker, you may double all ingredients.

ISLANDER CHICKEN DRUMSTICKS

Kids will love the sweetness of pineapple combined with their favorite chicken pieces. Busy cooks will love the ease of preparation for this delicious meal!

¾ cup apricot-pineapple jam
2 Tbs. soy sauce
1 tsp. ground ginger
1 tsp. lemon zest, grated
3 lbs. chicken drumsticks
¾ cup canned pineapple wedges, drained

For a 5, 6 or 7-quart Crock-Pot® slow cooker, double all ingredients.

In a small mixing bowl, combine the jam, soy sauce, ginger and lemon zest. Dip each drumstick into this mixture and place into the Crock-Pot® slow cooker. Pour the remaining jam mixture over the drumsticks. Add the pineapple chunks and mix thoroughly. Cover; cook on Low 4 to 6 hours (or on High for 2 to 3 hours). Remove the drumsticks and pineapple from the stoneware and place on a broiling tray. Broil for 10 minutes or until the chicken has browned. Makes 6 servings.

PIZZA PASTA

4 cups corkscrew pasta, cooked al denté and drained

15 slices salami, sliced into thin strips

4 fresh tomatoes, chopped

1 medium onion, chopped

1 green pepper, seeded and chopped

1–4 oz. can sliced black olives, drained

2 cloves garlic, minced

1 tsp. salt

1 tsp. dried oregano

½ tsp. dried rosemary

1 cup mozzarella cheese, grated

¼ cup Parmesan cheese

The flavors of a great salami and cheese pizza find their way into an easy dish for cooks on the go.

Combine all ingredients, except for the Parmesan cheese, in the Crock-Pot® slow cooker. Mix thoroughly. Cover; cook on Low 4 to 6 hours (or on High for 2 to 3 hours). Top with the Parmesan cheese. Cover and cook on High for another 15 minutes. Makes 6 servings.

You may double all the ingredients when using a 5, 6 or 7-quart Crock-Pot® slow cooker.

SLOPPY DOGS

This name says it all! Busy cooks can toss these ingredients into the Crock-Pot® slow cooker and know that dinner will be waiting when the family gets home.

8 to 10 hot dogs, chopped into 1-inch pieces
1–15 oz. can chili beans
1–6 oz. can tomato paste
¼ cup ketchup
1 small green bell pepper, chopped
1 small onion, finely chopped
1 tsp. prepared yellow mustard
1 Tbs. brown sugar
½ tsp. salt
½ tsp. chili powder
1 cup cheddar cheese, shredded
hamburger or hot dog buns

For a 5, 6 or 7-quart Crock-Pot® slow cooker, double all ingredients.

Combine all the ingredients, except the cheddar cheese and buns, in the Crock-Pot® slow cooker. Mix thoroughly. Cover; cook on Low 6 to 8 hours (or on High for 3 to 4 hours). Ten minutes before the end of cooking, stir in the cheddar cheese to melt slightly. Serve on hamburger or hot dog buns. Makes 6 servings.

EASY BARBECUE RIBS

3 lbs. beef or pork spareribs, sliced into serving pieces
1 tsp. salt
1 tsp. freshly ground black pepper
1 medium onion, sliced
1–14 oz. bottle of your favorite barbecue sauce
1 Tbs. brown sugar
2 Tbs. fresh lemon juice

These savory ribs will fall off the bone as they absorb the flavors of your favorite barbecue sauce.

Rub the spareribs with salt and pepper and broil for 15 minutes until browned. Place the spareribs and onion into the Crock-Pot® slow cooker. Combine the barbecue sauce, sugar, and lemon juice and pour over the ribs. Cover; cook on Low 8 to 10 hours (or on High for 4 to 5 hours). Makes 4 servings.

For a 5, 6 or 7-quart Crock-Pot® slow cooker, double all ingredients, except for the barbecue sauce.

BARBECUED CHICKEN PIZZA

Cook the chicken the night before this dish is to be served for a super-fast meal the next day. Barbecued Chicken Pizza can also be served as an appetizer for your Super Bowl party or holiday gathering. Improvise by adding your favorite pizza toppings.

2 to 3 lbs. chicken fryer pieces
1–14 oz. bottle of your favorite barbecue sauce
1–8 oz. can tomato sauce, with Italian seasonings
2 large pre-cooked pizza crusts
3 cups mozzarella cheese, shredded
¼ cup sweet red onion, thinly sliced
2 Tbs. fresh oregano, minced

For a 5, 6 or 7-quart Crock-Pot® slow cooker, double all ingredients, except for the barbecue sauce.

In the Crock-Pot® slow cooker, place the chicken fryer pieces with ¾ of the bottle of the barbecue sauce. Mix well to combine thoroughly. Cover; cook on Low 6 to 8 hours (or on High for 3 to 4 hours). Remove the chicken and let cool. Remove the meat from the bones and shred into bite-sized pieces. In a small bowl, combine the remaining barbecue sauce with the tomato sauce. Using a brush, spread the sauce over the pizza crusts, as desired. Top each pizza with the mozzarella cheese, shredded chicken and sliced red onion. Bake in the oven according to the pizza crust instructions. Makes 6 servings.

ALL-AMERICAN MEATLOAF

1½ lbs. lean ground turkey
2 cups bread crumbs
1 cup ketchup
½ cup onion, chopped
2 eggs, beaten
1 tsp. salt
1 tsp. freshly ground black pepper
8 slices cheddar or American cheese, each cut into 2 strips
2 Tbs. tomato paste

In a large mixing bowl, combine all the ingredients, except for the cheese and tomato paste. Shape half of the meat mixture into a loaf. Arrange 8 cheese strips on the meat, and top with the remaining meat, pressing the edges together to seal. Place in the Crock-Pot® slow cooker. Top with the tomato paste and remaining cheese slices. Cover; cook on Low 6 to 8 hours (or on High for 3 to 4 hours). Makes 6 servings.

A classic combination of meatloaf ingredients with a tomato and cheese twist!

You may double all the ingredients when using a 5, 6 or 7-quart Crock-Pot® slow cooker.

HOMESTYLE CHICKEN AND DUMPLINGS

Traditional, yet simple to prepare, this chicken and dumpling recipe is perfect for a cold winter evening meal.

1 medium onion, chopped
1½ lbs. fryer chicken parts
1 cup chicken broth
½ cup dry white wine
2 medium celery stalks, sliced
2 medium carrots, sliced
1 tsp. salt
½ tsp. freshly ground black pepper
½ cup frozen peas
½ cup heavy cream or milk
2 Tbs. flour
½ can refrigerated biscuits (5 biscuits)

In a large skillet, sauté the onion and chicken until browned. Place the skillet contents in the Crock-Pot® slow cooker. Add the remaining ingredients, except for the frozen peas, cream, flour and biscuits. Cover; cook on Low 6 to 8 hours (or on High for 3 to 4 hours). Let the chicken cool and remove the meat from the bones. Meanwhile, whisk together the cream and flour in a small bowl and stir into the slow cooker to thicken the stew. Cut each biscuit into 4 pieces. Drop these pieces into the stoneware and turn to High for 30 minutes. Return the chicken to the stew. Serve in individual bowls, ladling a couple of dumplings with the chicken in each serving. Makes 5 servings.

For a 5, 6 or 7-quart Crock-Pot® slow cooker, double the amount of chicken, chicken broth, and refrigerated biscuits.

CHICKEN CHOW MEIN

"Take-out" Chinese noodles right in your own Crock-Pot® slow cooker! Serve this with an Asian coleslaw (use an Asian bottled dressing instead of the traditional creamy dressing) and fortune cookies for an extra treat.

4 boneless, skinless chicken breasts, cut into 1½-inch pieces
½ cup water
1 medium onion, chopped
2 medium celery stalks, cut on the bias into ½-inch slices
2 Tbs. flour
3 Tbs. soy sauce
2 cloves garlic, minced
1 Tbs. brown sugar
1 Tbs. sesame oil
1–5 oz. can bamboo shoots, drained
1–6 oz. can sliced water chestnuts, drained
1 cup fresh bean sprouts
½ cup snow peas, trimmed
2 oz. cooked ham, finely shredded
4 green onions, finely sliced
*12 oz. chow mein noodles or linguine noodles, cooked al denté and
    drained*

In the Crock-Pot® slow cooker, combine the chicken, water, onion and celery. Cover; cook on Low 6 to 8 hours (or on High for 3 to 4 hours). In a small bowl, whisk together the flour, soy sauce, garlic, brown sugar and sesame oil. Add this and the bamboo shoots, water chestnuts, bean sprouts, snow peas and ham to the stoneware and turn to High. After one hour, add the green onions and mix thoroughly. Serve immediately over the hot noodles. Makes 6 servings.

For a 5, 6 or 7-quart Crock-Pot® slow cooker, double all ingredients.

HOP SING SWEET AND SOUR PORK

Serve this delightful dish over steamed white rice. The rich sauce will delight your tastebuds!

2 lbs. lean pork shoulder, cut into strips
1 green bell pepper, seeded and cut into strips
1 medium onion, thinly sliced
1 medium celery stalk, sliced on the bias
1 medium carrot, sliced on the bias
6 button mushrooms, thinly sliced
¼ cup brown sugar
1–8 oz. can tomato sauce
2 Tbs. cider vinegar
1 Tbs. soy sauce
1 tsp. salt
2 Tbs. cornstarch
1–14 oz. can pineapple chunks, with 1 cup juice reserved

Place the pork, bell pepper, onion, celery, carrot and mushrooms in the Crock-Pot® slow cooker. In a medium bowl, whisk together the brown sugar, tomato sauce, cider vinegar, soy sauce, salt and cornstarch, and add 1 cup of the pineapple juice. Pour this sauce over the contents of the stoneware. Cover; cook on Low 6 to 8 hours (or on High for 3 to 4 hours). One hour before serving, add the pineapple chunks to the pork and mix thoroughly. Makes 6 servings.

You may double all the ingredients when using a 5, 6 or 7-quart Crock-Pot® slow cooker.

STUFFED CABBAGE LEAVES

A popular recipe around the world, this easy dish combines interesting flavors with a fun presentation.

1 lb. ground beef
½ cup cooked rice
1 tsp. salt
½ tsp. freshly ground black pepper
2 tsp. fresh thyme, minced
2 tsp. fresh Italian parsley, minced
¼ tsp. ground nutmeg
¼ tsp. ground cinnamon
12 large cabbage leaves, blanched until pliable
1–6 oz. can tomato paste
¾ cup dry white wine

For a 5, 6 or 7-quart Crock-Pot® slow cooker, you may double all ingredients, except for the tomato paste and white wine.

In a mixing bowl, combine all the ingredients, except for the cabbage leaves, tomato paste and white wine. Place 2 Tbs. of the meat mixture in each cabbage leaf and roll to form a package. Place each roll into the Crock-Pot® slow cooker. In a small mixing bowl, whisk together the tomato paste and white wine. Pour over the cabbage rolls. Cover; cook on Low 8 to 10 hours (or on High for 4 to 5 hours). Makes 4 servings.

CLASSIC BAKED BEANS

3–16 oz. cans baked beans, drained
1 medium onion, chopped
¼ cup molasses
½ cup ketchup
¼ tsp. dry mustard
½ tsp. freshly ground black pepper
1 Tbs. Worcestershire sauce
6 slices bacon, crisply fried and crumbled

Serve with honeyed cornbread for instant satisfaction.

Place all ingredients in the Crock-Pot® slow cooker and mix thoroughly to combine. Cover; cook on Low 8 to 10 hours (or on High for 4 to 5 hours). Serves 6.

You may double all the ingredients when using a 5, 6 or 7-quart Crock-Pot® slow cooker.

CHAPTER 8

LOWFAT CROCK-POT®
SLOW COOKER MEALS
FOR HEALTHY LIVING

Most of us are careful about the amount of fat we consume in our diet, so we have created a chapter especially focused on lowfat recipes for the Crock-Pot® slow cooker. Your slow cooker is an ideal tool for healthy cooking because slow-cooking extracts exceptional flavor from meats and vegetables without adding fat or other unhealthy flavor enhancers. Instead of using butter or olive oil, our recipes substitute zesty combinations of fresh herbs and other seasonings to highlight the slow-cooked meats and vegetables. For example, our Citrus Beef Stew uses the fresh, bright flavors of orange to enhance an otherwise typical beef dish. Likewise, our Cool Chicken Curry Salad employs a variety of spices to create a soothing summer meal. We are excited to share recipes that are nutritious, simple to prepare, and, of course, delicious!

PARSNIP AND CARROT SOUP

This dish is a great year-round accompaniment to a main course of roasted meat. Or, the soup can stand alone as a quick, but satisfying meal in its own right.

For a 5, 6 or 7-quart Crock-Pot® slow cooker, double all ingredients.

1 medium leek, thinly sliced
4 medium parsnips, peeled and diced
4 medium carrots, peeled and diced
4 cups nonfat chicken stock
1 bay leaf
½ tsp. salt
½ tsp. freshly ground pepper
½ cup small pasta, cooked al denté and drained
1 Tbs. Italian parsley, chopped
1 cup lowfat croutons

In a small skillet, sauté the leek until golden. Drain and place in the Crock-Pot® slow cooker. Add the remaining ingredients except for the pasta, parsley and croutons. Cover; cook on Low 6 to 9 hours or until the vegetables are tender (or on High for 2 to 4 hours). Add the pasta during the last hour of cooking. Sprinkle each individual serving with a garnish of parsley and croutons. Makes 4 servings; 2 grams fat per serving.

CHICKEN & FRESH VEGETABLE NOODLE SOUP

2 medium onions, chopped
3 medium carrots, sliced
2 stalks of celery, sliced
2 to 3 lbs. whole fryer chicken, cleaned
1 cup noodles of your choice, cooked al denté and drained
2 Tbs. dried parsley
1 tsp. salt
¼ tsp. pepper
4 cups chicken broth
1 Tbs. fresh Italian parsley, minced
2 Tbs. fresh lemon juice

This nourishing dish is perfect on a cold day or simply when you want a little comfort. The addition of lemon juice and fresh parsley gives it a bright, fresh flavor.

Combine all ingredients, except the fresh Italian parsley and lemon juice, in the Crock-Pot® slow cooker. Cover; cook on Low 6 to 8 hours (or on High for 2-3 hours). Remove the chicken from the stoneware and let cool slightly; then remove the chicken meat from the bones. Discard the bones and return the chicken meat to the Crock-Pot® stoneware. Cover; cook on High for 30 minutes. Skim any fat from the top of the soup. Shortly before serving, add the Italian parsley and fresh lemon juice. Makes 8 servings; 8 grams of fat per serving.

For a 5, 6 or 7-quart Crock-Pot® slow cooker, you may double all ingredients.

SPICED LENTIL SOUP

Satisfying lentils combine with fresh vegetables for a healthy one-dish meal.

1 cup lentils, rinsed

1–28 oz. can stewed tomatoes, undrained

2 medium potatoes, diced

2 medium carrots, sliced

1 medium onion, chopped

1 celery stalk, sliced

3 cloves garlic, minced

3 bay leaves

3 Tbs. curry powder

1 tsp. salt

1 tsp. freshly ground black pepper

1 tsp. ground cumin

1 tsp. ground coriander

4 cups lowfat, low-sodium chicken or vegetable broth

Combine all the ingredients in the Crock-Pot® slow cooker. Cover; cook on Low 8 to 10 hours (or on High for 4 to 5 hours), or until lentils are tender. Remove the bay leaves before serving. Makes 4 to 6 servings; 1 gram of fat per serving.

For a 5, 6 or 7-quart Crock-Pot® slow cooker, double all ingredients.

CHICKEN BREASTS WITH WILD MUSHROOMS

This rich and elegant dish is surprisingly also lowfat!

6 skinless, boneless chicken breasts
1 tsp. fresh lemon juice
1 tsp. freshly ground black pepper
1 tsp. salt
1 tsp. garlic powder
1–10¾ oz. can fat-free cream of chicken soup
1–10¾ oz. can fat-free cream of mushroom soup
8 cremini mushrooms, sliced
2 shiitake mushrooms, sliced
2 Tbs. dried porcini mushrooms
1 Tbs. fresh Italian parsley, minced
1 clove garlic, minced
1–16 oz. package eggless noodles, cooked al denté and drained

Season the chicken breasts with the lemon juice, pepper, salt and garlic powder. Place in the Crock-Pot® slow cooker. In a medium mixing bowl, combine the soups, mushrooms, parsley and garlic. Pour the sauce over the chicken breasts in the stoneware. Cover; cook on Low 6 to 8 hours (or on High for 3 to 4 hours). Serve each chicken breast over a bed of noodles, with the sauce drizzled on top. Makes 6 servings; 3 grams of fat per serving.

You may double all the ingredients, except the soups, when using a 5, 6 or 7-quart Crock-Pot® slow cooker.

CAJUN CHICKEN & SHRIMP CREOLE

Enjoy the full flavors of chicken, shrimp and spices in this delicious creole!

2 lbs. skinless chicken thighs
1 red bell pepper, chopped
1 large onion, chopped
2 stalks celery, diced
1–15 oz. can stewed tomatoes, undrained and chopped
3 cloves garlic, minced
1 Tbs. granulated sugar
1 tsp. paprika
1 tsp. Cajun seasoning
1 tsp. salt
1 tsp. freshly ground black pepper
1 lb. shelled shrimp, deveined and cleaned
1 Tbs. fresh lemon juice
Louisiana hot sauce to taste
2 cups prepared quick-cooking rice

Place the chicken thighs in the bottom of the Crock-Pot® slow cooker. Add the remaining ingredients except for the shrimp, lemon juice, hot sauce and rice. Cover; cook on Low 8 to 10 hours (or on High for 4 to 5 hours). In the last hour of cooking, add the shrimp, lemon juice and hot sauce. Serve over the hot rice. Makes 6 servings; 6 grams of fat per serving.

For a 5, 6 or 7-quart Crock-Pot® slow cooker, double all ingredients.

HERBED ARTICHOKE CHICKEN

Inviting flavors of tomato, artichokes, Greek olives and herbs imbue the chicken and tease the appetite!

1½ lbs. skinless, boneless chicken breasts
1–14 oz. can tomatoes, drained and diced
1–14 oz. can artichoke hearts in water, drained
1 small onion, chopped
½ cup kalamata olives, pitted and sliced
1 cup nonfat chicken broth
¼ cup dry white wine
3 Tbs. quick cooking tapioca
2 tsp. curry powder
1 Tbs. fresh Italian parsley, chopped
1 tsp. dried sweet basil
1 tsp. dried thyme leaves
½ tsp. salt
½ tsp. freshly ground black pepper

Combine all the ingredients in the Crock-Pot® slow cooker. Mix thoroughly. Cover; cook on Low 6 to 8 hours (or on High for 3½ to 4 hours). Makes 6 servings; 4 grams of fat per serving.

For a 5, 6 or 7-quart Crock-Pot® slow cooker, double all ingredients, except for the chicken broth and white wine. Increase the chicken broth and white wine by one-half.

HALIBUT WITH TOMATO TAPENADE

The tomato tapenade lends a fresh taste to the halibut and is especially delicious when served over rice.

2 packages (12 oz. each) frozen or fresh halibut steaks
    (or any other firm white fish)
½ tsp. salt
½ tsp. freshly ground black pepper
2 medium tomatoes, chopped
¼ cup fresh lime juice
1 tsp. lemon zest, grated
2 Tbs. fresh basil, chopped
2 Tbs. fresh Italian parsley, minced
1 Tbs. extra-virgin olive oil
2 Tbs. capers, drained
2 cloves garlic, chopped

You may double all the ingredients when using a 5, 6 or 7-quart Crock-Pot® slow cooker.

Lightly coat the Crock-Pot® slow cooker with a non-fat cooking spray. Season the halibut with the salt and pepper, and place in the stoneware. In a small bowl, combine the tomatoes, lime juice, lemon zest, basil, parsley, olive oil, capers and garlic. Pour the tomatoes and sauce over the halibut. Cover; cook on High 2½ to 3 hours. Makes 6 servings; 4 grams of fat per serving.

MEDITERRANEAN TURKEY AND TOMATO RICE BAKE

2 cups uncooked converted long-grain rice

1½ lbs. skinless turkey breast, cut into bite-sized chunks

2 cups lowfat, low-sodium chicken broth

¼ cup Italian parsley, chopped

¼ cup black olives, sliced

¼ cup onion, finely chopped

1 clove garlic, minced

1 tsp. lemon zest, grated

1 Tbs. fresh lemon juice

1–14½ oz. can stewed tomatoes, undrained

¼ cup lowfat Parmesan cheese, grated

Combine all the ingredients in the Crock-Pot® slow cooker, except for the Parmesan cheese. Mix thoroughly. Cover; cook on Low 6 to 8 hours (or on High for 3 to 4 hours). Sprinkle with Parmesan cheese before serving. Makes 6 servings; 5 grams of fat per serving.

Healthy and flavorful, this turkey dish evokes the tastes of the sun-drenched Mediterranean.

For a 5, 6 or 7-quart Crock-Pot® slow cooker, double all ingredients.

HERB-SPRINKLED SCALLOPED POTATOES

Usually filled with cream and butter, these scalloped potatoes are a healthy alternative.

1 medium onion, thinly sliced
2 cloves garlic, minced
1 Tbs. extra-virgin olive oil
salt & pepper to taste
½ tsp. freshly ground black pepper
¼ tsp. salt
2 Tbs. flour
3 lbs. Yukon Gold potatoes, peeled and thinly sliced
2 cups lowfat milk
1 cup lowfat, low-sodium chicken broth
3 Tbs. chives or green onions, minced
3 Tbs. fresh Italian parsley, minced

Lightly coat the Crock-Pot® slow cooker with a non-fat cooking spray. In a medium skillet, sauté the onion and garlic in the olive oil until soft. Season with salt and pepper. Combine the black pepper, salt and flour in a small bowl. Dredge the potato slices in this mixture and cover the bottom of the slow cooker with about one-third of the potatoes. Spread with half the onion mixture. Continue with the layers, ending with a top layer of potatoes. Pour the milk and broth over the potatoes. Cover; cook on Low for 7 to 9 hours (or on High for 3 to 4 hours). Sprinkle with the chives and parsley before serving. Makes 6 side servings; 4 grams of fat per serving.

You may double all the ingredients when using a 5, 6 or 7-quart Crock-Pot® slow cooker, except for the milk and chicken broth. Increase the milk and chicken broth by one-half.

SUMMER'S BOUNTY CHICKEN & FRESH VEGETABLES

Serve over fluffy, white rice for an easy summertime meal.

6 skinless, boneless chicken breasts
1 tsp. salt
1 tsp. freshly ground black pepper
¼ cup orange juice concentrate, thawed
1 Tbs. honey
3 Tbs. fresh basil, chopped
1 clove garlic, minced
2 red bell peppers, seeded and chopped
2 zucchini, sliced
1–14 oz. can pineapple chunks, packed in natural juices, drained

Season the chicken breasts with the salt and pepper and place in the Crock-Pot® slow cooker. In a small bowl, combine the orange juice concentrate, honey, basil and garlic. Add the peppers, zucchini and pineapple chunks to the stoneware, and pour the orange juice sauce on top of all the other ingredients. Cover; cook on Low 6 to 8 hours (or on High for 3 to 4 hours). Makes 6 servings; 2 grams of fat per serving.

You may double all the ingredients when using a 5, 6 or 7-quart Crock-Pot® slow cooker.

CRAB & SPINACH LASAGNE

This delightful dish is surprisingly low in fat. Enjoy!

1 large onion, chopped

2 medium carrots, diced

2 cloves garlic, minced

16 oz. lump crabmeat, shredded

1–10 oz. package frozen chopped spinach, thawed and squeezed dry

1 Tbs. fresh oregano, minced

2 Tbs. fresh Italian parsley, minced

1 Tbs. fresh thyme, minced

1 tsp. salt

1 tsp. freshly ground black pepper

1-10 oz. package broad lasagne noodles, cooked al denté, drained and cut into thirds

White Sauce

2 Tbs. margarine, melted

2 Tbs. all-purpose flour

1 tsp. salt

1 cup nonfat milk

2 cups shredded lowfat mozzarella, divided

1–12 oz. carton nonfat cottage cheese

In a medium skillet, sauté the onion, carrots and garlic until tender. Add the crabmeat and spinach, and season with the oregano, parsley, thyme, salt and pepper. Transfer the crab mixture to the Crock-Pot® slow cooker. Add the lasagne noodles. In a medium mixing bowl, combine the margarine, flour, salt, milk, 1 cup of the mozzarella cheese, and the cottage cheese. Pour the white sauce over the lasagne in the stoneware. Cover; cook on Low 4 to 6 hours (or on High for 2 to 3 hours). Thirty minutes before the end of cooking, top the lasagne with the remaining mozzarella cheese and turn to High. Makes 8 to 10 servings; 5 grams of fat per serving.

For a 5, 6 or 7-quart Crock-Pot® slow cooker, double all ingredients except for the White Sauce ingredients. Increase the sauce ingredients by one-half.

TRI-PEPPER SOUTHWESTERN PENNE

A lively and colorful presentation of vegetables, herbs and pasta!

1 large onion, chopped

2 cloves garlic, minced

8 button mushrooms, sliced

1 tsp. dried oregano

1 tsp. dried thyme

1 tsp. dried sweet basil

1 tsp. dried parsley

1 medium red bell pepper, sliced

1 medium yellow bell pepper, sliced

1 medium green bell pepper, sliced

1 tsp. salt

1 tsp. freshly ground black pepper

1–14½ oz. can stewed tomatoes, chopped

1–6 oz. can tomato sauce

1 cup water

2 tsp. granulated sugar

2 Tbs. dry white wine

1 cup frozen or fresh kernel corn

1–4 oz. can sliced black olives

1 lb. penne pasta, cooked al denté and drained

In a medium skillet, sauté the onion, garlic and mushrooms until soft. Add the oregano, thyme, sweet basil and parsley. Transfer the vegetables and herbs to the Crock-Pot® slow cooker. Add the remaining ingredients, except for the pasta, and mix thoroughly to combine. Cover; cook on Low 4 to 6 hours (or on High for 2 to 3 hours). To serve, place the pasta on six individual plates and spoon the sauce on top of the pasta. Makes 6 servings; 3 grams of fat per serving.

For a 5, 6 or 7-quart Crock-Pot® slow cooker, double all ingredients.

CHICKEN POT AU FEU

This classic French dish is full of flavor and is incredibly easy to make.

2 medium carrots, cut into ½-inch slices
1 medium onion, cut in half
2 medium celery stalks, cut into 1-inch pieces
2 medium new potatoes, cut into ¼-inch pieces
3 lbs. broiler/fryer chicken
1 tsp. salt
½ tsp. freshly ground black pepper
½ cup water
1 tsp. dried bay leaves
1 tsp. dried basil
1 tsp. dried thyme

You may double all the ingredients when using a 5, 6 or 7-quart Crock-Pot® slow cooker.

Place the carrots, onion, celery and potatoes in the bottom of the Crock-Pot® slow cooker. Add the whole chicken. Top with the remaining ingredients. Cover; cook on Low 8 to 10 hours (or on High for 3½ to 5 hours). Remove the chicken and vegetables and arrange attractively on a platter before serving. Makes 5 servings; 12 grams of fat per serving.

Note: You may strain the broth and use as chicken stock for future cooking.

COOL CHICKEN CURRY SALAD

3 lbs. whole broiler/fryer chicken
1 tsp. salt
½ tsp. freshly ground black pepper
½ cup nonfat mayonnaise
½ tsp. cayenne pepper
2½ Tbs. curry powder
½ tsp. garlic powder
½ tsp. salt

2 Tbs. mango chutney
1 small green apple, cored and finely chopped
2 medium stalks celery, finely sliced
3 green onions, finely sliced
¼ cup golden raisins (optional)
¼ cup sliced almonds (optional)

Cook the chicken in your Crock-Pot® slow cooker the night before you serve this salad. Perfect for a warm summer's evening when only something refreshing and mellow will do.

Season the chicken with the salt and pepper and place in the Crock-Pot® slow cooker. Pour ¼ cup water into the stoneware. Cover; cook on Low 8 to 10 hours (or on High for 3½ to 5 hours). Remove the chicken from the stoneware and, when cooled, remove the chicken meat from the bones. Cut into ½-inch pieces. Combine 3 cups of the chicken with the remaining ingredients. If you prefer, you may add additional nonfat mayonnaise. Serve over butter lettuce leaves. Makes 4 side-servings; 18 grams fat per serving.

You may double all ingredients for the 5, 6 or 7-quart Crock-Pot® slow cooker.

BRAISED WINTER SQUASH

The sweet, earthy flavors of squash are accented by the soy sauce and honey in this recipe. Drizzle the sauce over sticky white rice for another flavorful side dish.

2 Acorn or Kabocha squashes (approximately 1½ lbs. each)
3 Tbs. reduced-sodium soy sauce
1 cup vegetable stock or water
3 Tbs. honey
3 Tbs. sake or dry white wine

For a 5, 6 or 7-quart Crock-Pot® slow cooker, double all ingredients.

Cut each squash in half and scoop out and discard the seeds. Cut the squash into 2 to 3-inch pieces. Place in the Crock-Pot® slow cooker. In a small bowl, whisk together the remaining ingredients and pour over the squash. Cover; cook on Low 8 to 10 hours (or on High for 2½ to 4 hours.) Remove the squash from the sauce to serve. Makes 6 to 8 side servings; less than 1 gram of fat per serving.

LAMB WITH BALSAMIC-GLAZED VEGETABLES

1 tsp. salt

1 tsp. freshly ground black pepper

1 tsp. ground coriander

2 tsp. dried rosemary leaves

1 tsp. dried mint

1 tsp. dried thyme

1 tsp. ground fennel

3 lbs. lamb roast, de-boned and well-trimmed of fat

1 large red onion, cut into eighths

2 medium zucchini, bias-cut into ½-inch slices

2 yellow crookneck squash, bias-cut into ½-inch slices

2 medium new potatoes, quartered

3 Tbs. balsamic vinegar

Well-seasoned lamb is balanced by the tart sweetness of the balsamic vinegar glaze and vegetables.

Combine the salt, pepper, coriander, rosemary, mint, thyme and fennel in a small bowl. Rub the seasonings all over the lamb roast. Place the onion in the bottom of the Crock-Pot® slow cooker and add the lamb roast. Add the remaining vegetables. Drizzle the balsamic vinegar over the vegetables. Cover and cook on High for 1 hour, then turn to Low for 10 to 12 hours. Makes 8 servings; 17 grams of fat per serving.

For a 5, 6 or 7-quart Crock-Pot® slow cooker, double all the ingredients.

CITRUS BEEF STEW

The full flavors of beef are brightened by the fresh taste of orange.

1 cup onion, finely chopped
1 cup carrots, finely chopped
1 cup celery, finely chopped
2 Tbs. tomato paste
1 cup nonfat beef stock
¼ cup fresh Italian parsley, chopped
½ cup red wine
½ cup orange juice
3 strips orange zest
1½ lbs. beef chuck, cut into 1½-inch cubes
1 cup butternut squash, cut into 1½-inch cubes
1 cup new potatoes, quartered
1 cup green beans, trimmed
1 tsp. salt
½ tsp. freshly ground black pepper
1 bay leaf

In a large skillet, sauté the onion, carrot and celery until tender. Place in the Crock-Pot® slow cooker. In a small bowl, whisk the tomato paste into the beef stock. Add to the vegetables. Add the remaining ingredients to the stoneware. Cover; cook on Low 8 to 10 hours (or on High for 4 to 5 hours). Makes 6 servings; 15 grams of fat per serving.

For a 5, 6 or 7-quart Crock-Pot® slow cooker, double all ingredients.

BEAN AND CORN CHILI

Hearty yet lowfat, this chili will warm you on any winter evening.

2 medium onions, finely chopped
5 cloves garlic, minced
½ tsp. olive oil
2 Tbs. red wine
1 green bell pepper, seeded and finely chopped
1 red bell pepper, seeded and finely chopped
2 stalks celery, finely sliced
6 Roma tomatoes, chopped
2–15 oz. cans kidney beans, rinsed and drained
1–6 oz. can tomato paste
8 oz. frozen corn kernels
1 tsp. salt
1 tsp. chili powder
½ tsp. freshly ground black pepper
¼ tsp. cumin
¼ tsp. cayenne pepper
¼ tsp. dried oregano
¼ tsp. ground coriander
1½ cups nonfat chicken or vegetable broth

In a medium skillet, sauté the onions and garlic in the olive oil and red wine. Add the skillet contents and the remaining ingredients to the Crock-Pot® slow cooker. Mix thoroughly. Cover; cook on Low 6 to 8 hours (or on High for 3 to 4 hours). Makes 6 servings; 3 grams of fat per serving.

For a 5, 6 or 7-quart Crock-Pot® slow cooker, double all ingredients.

BLACK BEAN STUFFED PEPPERS

Exciting flavors of Mexico! This lowfat, vegetarian entrée is perfect for any day of the week.

You may increase the recipe ingredients, except the tomato soup, for the 5, 6 or 7-quart Crock-Pot® slow cooker, however the peppers should fit comfortably in a single layer in your stoneware.

1 medium onion, finely chopped
¼ tsp. cayenne pepper
¼ tsp. dried oregano
¼ tsp. ground cumin
¼ tsp. chili powder
2–15 oz. cans black beans, rinsed and drained
6 tall green bell peppers, seeded and cored
1 cup reduced-fat Jack cheese, grated
1 cup tomato salsa
½ cup fat-free sour cream

In a medium skillet, sauté the onion until golden. Season with the cayenne pepper, oregano, cumin and chili powder. In a medium mixing bowl, mash half of the black beans with the sautéed onions. Mix in the remaining beans. Place the bell peppers in the Crock-Pot® slow cooker, and spoon the black bean mixture into the bell peppers. Sprinkle the cheese over the peppers. Pour the salsa over the cheese. Cover; cook on Low 6 to 8 hours (or on High for 3 to 4 hours). Serve each pepper with a dollop of sour cream. Makes 6 servings; 7 grams of fat per serving.

CHICKEN AND SWEET POTATO STEW

4 boneless, skinless chicken breasts, cut into bite-sized pieces
2 medium sweet potatoes, peeled and cubed
2 medium Yukon Gold potatoes, peeled and cubed
2 medium carrots, peeled and cut into ½-inch slices
1–28 oz. can whole stewed tomatoes
1 tsp. salt
½ tsp. freshly ground black pepper
⅛ tsp. ground cinnamon
⅛ tsp. ground nutmeg
1 tsp. paprika
1 tsp. celery seed
¼ cup fresh basil, chopped
1 cup nonfat, low sodium chicken broth

Combine all ingredients in the Crock-Pot® slow cooker. Cover; cook on Low for 6 to 8 hours (or on High for 3 to 4 hours). Makes 6 servings; 3 grams of fat per serving.

This light stew has an Indian influence and offers excellent flavor without the fat.

You may double all the ingredients when using a 5, 6 or 7-quart Crock-Pot® slow cooker.

CHINESE HOT POT

A savory Chinese soup chock full of fresh, tasty ingredients! This soup is especially comforting when your immune system is stressed.

½ lb. stew beef, cut into chunks
2 medium zucchini, sliced
8 button mushrooms, cut in half
1 cup broccoli flowerets
1 cup extra-firm tofu, cut into cubes
3 cups vegetable broth
3 cloves garlic, minced
1 Tbs. fresh ginger, grated
3 Tbs. low-sodium soy sauce
1 tsp. red pepper flakes
1 tsp. sesame oil
1 Tbs. honey
½ cup bean sprouts
½ cup sugar snap peas, trimmed
1–4 oz. can water chestnuts, drained

In the Crock-Pot® slow cooker, combine all the ingredients except for the bean sprouts, snap peas and water chestnuts. Mix thoroughly. Cover; cook on Low 6 to 8 hours (or on High for 3 to 4 hours). Thirty minutes before the end of cooking, add the bean sprouts, snap peas, and water chestnuts to the stoneware. Makes 4 servings; 9 grams of fat per serving.

For a 5, 6 or 7-quart Crock-Pot® slow cooker, you may double all the ingredients.

TUSCAN VEGETABLE TORTE

Italy offers the best of her bounty in this delicious entrée. If desired, you may use a food processor to speed the slicing process.

3 medium potatoes, sliced

1 medium onion, sliced

2 medium carrots, sliced on the bias

1 red bell pepper, seeded and sliced into rings

1 medium zucchini, sliced on the bias

1 cup fresh or frozen kernel corn

1 cup skim mozzarella cheese, shredded

2 cups tomato sauce

1 Tbs. soy sauce

1 Tbs. fresh Italian parsley, minced

1 Tbs. fresh thyme leaves, minced

1 Tbs. fresh basil leaves, chopped

1 tsp. salt

½ tsp. freshly ground black pepper

½ tsp. ground cinnamon

Coat the Crock-Pot® slow cooker with a non-fat, non-stick cooking spray. Layer the vegetables in the order given, sprinkling a little of the mozzarella cheese between each layer. In a medium mixing bowl, combine the tomato sauce, soy sauce, parsley, thyme, basil, salt, pepper and cinnamon. Pour this sauce over the layered vegetables. Top with any remaining mozzarella cheese. Cover; cook on Low 8 to 10 hours (or on High for 4 to 5 hours). Makes 6 servings; 1 gram of fat per serving.

For a 5, 6 or 7-quart Crock-Pot® slow cooker, double all ingredients, except for the sauce ingredients, which should be increased by one-half.

TOMATO & BASIL ZITI WITH ROASTED VEGETABLES

Bursting with full-bodied flavors, this entrée is excellent on any night of the week.

1 medium red onion, roughly chopped

1 yellow bell pepper, seeded and chopped

1 medium carrot, julienned

1 cup prepared tomato and basil pasta sauce

1–10 oz. package frozen spinach, defrosted and drained

1–14 oz. can tomatoes, undrained and crushed

1–8 oz. can tomato sauce

1 shallot, minced

2 cloves garlic, minced

½ tsp. crushed red pepper

1 tsp. salt

½ tsp. freshly ground black pepper

½ tsp. sugar

½ tsp. ground thyme

½ tsp. ground sage

3 Tbs. fresh Italian parsley, chopped

1 cup lowfat mozzarella cheese, grated

16 oz. ziti pasta, cooked al denté and drained

Combine all of the ingredients, except for the mozzarella cheese and pasta, in the Crock-Pot® slow cooker. Cover; cook on Low 6 to 8 hours (or on High for 3 to 4 hours). For each individual serving, place a serving of the pasta, sprinkled with the mozzarella cheese, in a pasta bowl, and then ladle the pasta sauce over the top. Makes 6 servings; 2 grams of fat per serving.

For a 5, 6 or 7-quart Crock-Pot® slow cooker, you may double all ingredients.

ASIAN LETTUCE WRAPS

This flavorful lowfat dish can be served as an appealing appetizer or a refreshing main course.

1½ lbs. extra-lean ground chicken or turkey
1 medium onion, finely chopped
2 medium celery stalks, chopped
½ cup hoisin sauce
3 Tbs. soy sauce
2 cloves garlic, minced
2 Tbs. fresh ginger, grated
1 Tbs. brown sugar
1 Tbs. sesame oil
½ Tbs. Asian chile paste
1–5 oz. can bamboo shoots, drained
2–6 oz. cans sliced water chestnuts, drained
1 cup fresh bean sprouts
4 green onions, finely sliced
¼ cup fresh cilantro, minced
14 crisp iceberg lettuce leaves
¼ cup hoisin sauce

In the Crock-Pot® slow cooker, combine the chicken, onion, celery, hoisin sauce, soy sauce, garlic, ginger, brown sugar, sesame oil, chile paste, bamboo shoots and water chestnuts. Cover; cook on Low 6 to 8 hours (or on High for 3 to 4 hours). Thirty minutes before the end of cooking, add the bean sprouts, green onions and cilantro. Mix thoroughly. To serve, place 2 tablespoons of the chicken mixture on an iceberg lettuce leaf and drizzle with hoisin sauce. Roll the filled lettuce leaf into a pocket-style sandwich. Serves 7; 7 grams of fat per serving.

For a 5, 6 or 7-quart Crock-Pot® slow cooker, double all ingredients.

CHAPTER 9

DELECTABLE CROCK-POT® SLOW COOKER DESSERT RECIPES

Not only is your Crock-Pot® slow cooker the place to cook the most savory of dishes, but it also is an excellent way to create mouth-watering desserts. From scrumptious cheesecakes to tasty fruit cobblers, your slow cooker offers you the ability to produce beautiful desserts with only a modicum of effort. Your family and guests will be truly amazed with the ease with which you will conjure up toothsome ways to complete your meals!

Included in this chapter are fabulous desserts that are beautiful enough to serve at the most elegant of dinner parties. From Cinnamon Ginger Poached Pears to Candied Bananas Foster, these desserts are both sophisticated and delicious. In addition, we have included homestyle favorites such as bread and rice puddings and other old-fashioned treats for families of all ages. Most importantly, all of these desserts require little effort to prepare and clean up is easy. You will soon be hearing accolades from your family and friends for your amazing Crock-Pot® slow cooker desserts!

Please note that the breads and cakes in this chapter can all be cooked in the stoneware. However, for best results, you should use the Crock-Pot® Bread 'N Cake Pan. You may purchase one by calling 1-800-577-4825 or at www.crock-pot.com.

COCONUT BREAD PUDDING

A twist on the old favorite, this dessert injects the sweet flavor of coconut and golden raisins into the otherwise traditional bread pudding.

1 cup unsweetened coconut milk
½ cup milk
1 cup lite evaporated milk
4 cups dry French bread with crust, cut into 1-inch cubes
2 large eggs
½ cup sugar
½ tsp. salt
1½ tsp. pure vanilla extract
½ cup firmly packed sweetened coconut flakes
½ cup golden raisins

You may double all the ingredients when using a 5, 6 or 7-quart Crock-Pot® slow cooker.

In a lightly greased Crock-Pot® slow cooker, combine the coconut milk, milk, evaporated milk and French bread pieces. Stir thoroughly to mix. In small mixing bowl, beat the eggs, sugar, salt and vanilla extract. Add the egg mixture to the bread and milk mixture in the stoneware. Stir in the coconut flakes and raisins. Cover; cook on High for 3 hours. Serve warm or chilled. Garnish with additional coconut flakes, if desired. Makes 6 to 8 servings.

CINNAMON GINGER POACHED PEARS

3 cups water

1 cup granulated sugar

10 slices fresh ginger

2 whole cinnamon sticks

6 Bosc or Anjou pears, peeled and cored

1 Tbs. candied ginger, minced, for garnish

In the Crock-Pot® slow cooker, combine the water, sugar, fresh ginger and cinnamon sticks. Place the pears in this mixture. Cover; cook on Low 4 to 6 hours (or on High for 1½ to 2 hours). Remove the pears from the sauce and let cool. Turn the slow cooker to High and heat, uncovered, for about 30 minutes to allow the liquid to reduce to a thick syrup. Drizzle this syrup over the pears. Garnish with the candied ginger.

Elegant, yet oh-so-simple, these poached pears are a delicious way to end a meal.

For a 5, 6 or 7-quart Crock-Pot® slow cooker, you may double all ingredients.

CHOCOLATE COFFEE BREAD PUDDING

Top this delicious dessert with a scoop of your favorite vanilla bean ice cream, dusted with cocoa powder.

1 cup butter
¼ cup sugar
1 tsp. ground cinnamon
4 eggs
1½ cup chocolate milk
¼ cup strong coffee
½ cup currants
½ cup raisins, optional
½ cup milk chocolate chips
1 cup chopped pecans, toasted
4 cups stale white bread, cut into bite-sized pieces

For a 5, 6 or 7-quart Crock-Pot® slow cooker, you may double all ingredients.

In a bowl, beat the butter, sugar and cinnamon with an electric mixer. Add the eggs and beat until fluffy. Mix in the chocolate milk, coffee, currants and raisins. Fold the chocolate chips, pecans and bread cubes into the mixture. Pour into a lightly greased Crock-Pot® slow cooker. Cover; cook on Low for 5 to 6 hours (or on High for 2½ to 3 hours).

BASIL AND CINNAMON SYRUP NECTARINES

1½ cups water
3 Tbs. sugar
½ cup fresh basil, finely shredded
1 cinnamon stick
8 fresh nectarines, pitted and cut in quarters
1 Tbs. fresh lemon juice

This dessert topping is a sophisticated and surprising blend of summer flavors. You can also substitute peaches for the nectarines.

Combine all ingredients, except for the lemon juice, in the Crock-Pot® slow cooker. Cook on High 2 to 3 hours. Remove the nectarines from the syrup and set aside. Let the syrup cool and then strain. Stir the lemon juice into the syrup. Put the nectarines back into the syrup and serve as a topping over your favorite cake or ice cream.

You may double all the ingredients when using a 5, 6 or 7-quart Crock-Pot® slow cooker.

ORANGE ALMOND RICE PUDDING

A refined take on rice pudding, this rice dessert employs a delicate combination of orange and almond, with the tangy sweetness of the Crème Fraiche Topping.

4 cups lite evaporated milk
¾ cup sugar
½ cup short-grain rice, cooked
⅓ cup golden raisins
⅓ cup almonds, toasted and roughly chopped
2 Tbs. orange zest, finely grated
1 Tbs. cornstarch
2 large eggs, beaten
1 tsp. almond extract
1 Tbs. brown sugar
½ tsp. ground cinnamon
¼ cup sliced almonds, toasted
1 tsp. candied orange zest

Crème Fraiche Topping
1 cup heavy cream, at room temperature
2 tsp. sour cream, at room temperature
2 Tbs. brown sugar
1 tsp. almond extract

To prepare the pudding, lightly grease the Crock-Pot® slow cooker. In a mixing bowl, combine the milk, sugar, rice, golden raisins, almonds, orange zest and cornstarch. Gradually add in the beaten eggs and almond extract. Pour into the stoneware. Sprinkle the brown sugar and cinnamon over the rice mixture. Cover; cook on High 2 to 3 hours or until the pudding is set. To serve, dollop the crème fraiche topping over individual bowls of pudding. (see Crème Fraiche Topping below). Sprinkle each serving with sliced almonds and candied orange zest. Makes 4 servings.

The Crème Fraiche Topping must be made one day ahead. To prepare, pour the heavy cream into a clean glass jar with a lid. Add the sour cream and place the lid on the jar. Shake the mixture to combine thoroughly. Let the mixture stand uncovered for 1 day, at room temperature. The Crème Fraiche Topping should thicken considerably. Once thickened, add the brown sugar and almond extract to the mixture. Mix thoroughly. Place the lid on the jar and refrigerate for at least 6 hours.

For a 5, 6 or 7-quart Crock-Pot® slow cooker, double all ingredients.

PEACH COBBLER
WITH LAVENDER SYRUP

The lavender syrup is a subtle and delectable addition to the traditional peach cobbler. You can find dried lavender blossoms in specialty food stores or in the organic section of your grocery store.

¾ cup all-purpose baking mix
⅓ cup granulated sugar
½ cup brown sugar
2 eggs
2 tsp. vanilla
2 tsp. butter, melted
½ can evaporated milk
3 large ripe peaches, sliced
¾ tsp. cinnamon

Lavender Syrup
1½ cups water
4 Tbs. golden honey
½ tsp. dried lavender blossoms
1 sprig fresh rosemary

Lightly grease the Crock-Pot® slow cooker. In a large mixing bowl, combine the baking mix, granulated sugar and brown sugar. Add the eggs and vanilla. Mix thoroughly. Pour in the butter and milk, and add the peaches and cinnamon, mixing until thoroughly combined. Pour into the stoneware. Cover and cook on Low 6 to 8 hours (or on High for 3 to 4 hours). Serve while still warm. Drizzle Lavender Syrup (see below) over each individual serving. Serves 4.

To prepare the Lavender Syrup, combine all syrup ingredients in a small pan. Simmer over low heat until reduced to 1 cup, about 15 minutes. Cool to room temperature and then strain.

For a 5, 6 or 7-quart Crock-Pot® slow cooker, you may double all ingredients.

STRAWBERRY AND RHUBARB PANDOWDY

The tartness of rhubarb accents the sweetness of strawberries in this scrumptious pandowdy.

Filling ingredients:
1½ lbs. rhubarb, diced into ½-inch pieces
1 pint strawberries, quartered
1 cup granulated sugar
1 Tbs. fresh lemon juice
2 tsp. lemon zest, grated

Topping ingredients:
¾ cup all-purpose baking mix
½ cup unsalted butter
¼ cup brown sugar

For a 5, 6 or 7-quart Crock-Pot® slow cooker, double all ingredients.

Lightly grease the Crock-Pot® slow cooker. In large mixing bowl, combine the fruit, granulated sugar, lemon juice and lemon zest. Pour into the stoneware. In a separate bowl, combine the baking mix, butter and brown sugar until a crumbly dough is formed. Sprinkle this dough over the fruit mixture, distributing evenly. Cover and cook on Low 6 to 8 hours (or on High for 3 to 4 hours). Serve warm, topped with your favorite ice cream, if desired.

CANDIED BANANAS FOSTER

6 green-tipped bananas, peeled and cut in quarters
½ cup flaked coconut
½ tsp. cinnamon
¼ tsp. salt
½ cup dark corn syrup
⅓ cup unsalted butter, melted
1 tsp. lemon zest, grated
3 Tbs. lemon juice
1 tsp. rum
12 slices pound cake, about 1-inch thick
1 qt. French vanilla ice cream, softened
confectioner's sugar, for garnish

Sure to be a family favorite, a show-stopping dessert doesn't get any easier than this!

Combine the bananas and coconut in the Crock-Pot® slow cooker. In a medium mixing bowl, combine the cinnamon, salt, corn syrup, butter, lemon zest, lemon juice and rum. Pour over the banana and coconut mixture. Cover; cook on Low 1 to 2 hours.

To create individual servings, place one scoop of the French vanilla ice cream between two slices of poundcake, like a sandwich. Ladle the bananas and sauce over each ice cream sandwich, and dust each with confectioner's sugar, for garnish. Makes 6 servings.

For a 5, 6 or 7-quart Crock-Pot® slow cooker, double all ingredients.

CLASSIC BAKED APPLES

*This traditional dish
is incredibly simple
to prepare.*

2 Tbs. golden raisins
¼ cup brown sugar
1 tsp. lemon zest, grated
6 small to medium baking apples, washed and cored
1 tsp. cinnamon
2 Tbs. butter
¼ cup orange juice
¼ cup water
whipped cream for garnish

For a 5, 6 or 7-
quart Crock-Pot®
slow cooker, double
all ingredients.

Mix the raisins, sugar and lemon zest and fill the cored center of each apple. Put the apples in the Crock-Pot® slow cooker. Sprinkle with the cinnamon and dot with the butter. Add the orange juice and water. Cover; cook on Low 7 to 9 hours (or on High for 2½ to 3½ hours). Serve with a dollop of whipped cream.

BANANA NUT BREAD

⅓ cup butter or margarine
⅔ cup granulated sugar
2 eggs, well beaten
2 Tbs. dark corn syrup
3 ripe bananas, well mashed
1¾ cup all-purpose flour, sifted
2 tsp. baking powder
¼ tsp. baking soda
½ tsp. salt
½ cup walnuts, shelled and chopped

Banana nut bread has always been a favorite way to use up those overripe bananas. Not only is it delicious, but it also freezes well for future use.

Grease and flour the inside of the stoneware or the Crock-Pot® Bread 'N Cake Bake Pan (available through Rival). In a large bowl, cream the butter until fluffy, and slowly add the sugar, eggs, corn syrup and mashed bananas. Beat until smooth. In a small bowl, sift together the flour, baking powder, baking soda and salt. Slowly beat the flour mixture into the creamed mixture. Add the walnuts and mix thoroughly. Pour into the bake pan and place in the Crock-Pot® slow cooker. Cover; cook on High for 2 to 3 hours. When the bread is done, remove the Bread 'N Cake Bake Pan from the stoneware. Let cool, and then turn bread out onto the serving platter. Makes 6 servings.

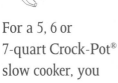

For a 5, 6 or 7-quart Crock-Pot® slow cooker, you may double all ingredients.

PUMPKIN SPICE CAKE

Perfect for a light dessert or as a morning treat with your coffee.

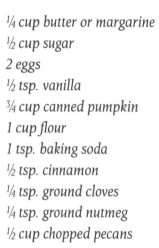

¼ cup butter or margarine
½ cup sugar
2 eggs
½ tsp. vanilla
¾ cup canned pumpkin
1 cup flour
1 tsp. baking soda
½ tsp. cinnamon
¼ tsp. ground cloves
¼ tsp. ground nutmeg
½ cup chopped pecans

It's best to make two of these delicious Pumpkin Spice Cakes separately rather than doubling the ingredients for the larger sizes of Crock-Pot® slow cookers.

Grease and flour the stoneware or the Crock-Pot® Bread N' Cake Pan (available through Rival). In a mixing bowl, cream the butter and sugar with an electric mixer. Add the eggs, vanilla and pumpkin, and beat well. Combine the flour, baking soda, cinnamon, cloves and nutmeg, and stir into the creamed mixture. Mix in the chopped pecans. Pour into the prepared bake pan and cover. Place in the slow cooker. Cover; cook on High 3 to 4 hours. When the cake is done, remove the Crock-Pot® Bread N' Cake Pan from the stoneware. Let cool, and then turn the cake out onto the serving platter. Makes 12 servings.

HOMESTYLE APPLE BROWN BETTY

6 cups of your favorite cooking apples, peeled, cored, and cut into eighths

3 cups bread crumbs

1 tsp. ground cinnamon

1 tsp. ground nutmeg

⅛ tsp. salt

¾ cup brown sugar

½ cup butter or margarine, melted

¼ cup walnuts, finely chopped

This recipe conjures up an amazing dessert out of simple ingredients.

Lightly grease the Crock-Pot® slow cooker. Place the apples in the bottom of the stoneware. In a mixing bowl, combine the bread crumbs, cinnamon, nutmeg, salt, brown sugar, butter and walnuts, and spread over the apples in the stoneware. Cover; cook on Low 3 to 4 hours. (or on High for 2 hours). Makes 8 servings.

For a 5, 6 or 7-quart Crock-Pot® slow cooker, double all ingredients.

RUSTIC CRANBERRY-APPLE BUTTER

This is a flavorful spread to use on toast in the morning, or as a topping on a dish of ice cream at night.

6 large cooking apples, cored, peeled, and thinly sliced
1 cup apple juice
½ cup fresh cranberries
1 large strip lemon zest
2 Tbs. fresh lemon juice
¾ cup sugar

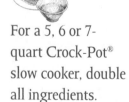

For a 5, 6 or 7-quart Crock-Pot® slow cooker, double all ingredients.

Combine all ingredients in the Crock-Pot® slow cooker. Mix thoroughly. Cover; cook on Low 8 to 10 hours (or on High for 4 to 5 hours). Stir about every 2 hours. Remove the cover after 3 hours to allow the fruit and juice to cook down. Spoon into sterilized jars and process according to standard canning methods.

STRAWBERRY-APRICOT SAUCE

1 cup dried apricot halves, cut into ½-inch strips
1 cup apricot juice or nectar
6 cups sliced strawberries
⅔ cup sugar
2 Tbs. fresh mint, minced
1 Tbs. fresh ginger, grated

An exquisite sauce to pour over ice cream or pound cake.

Combine all the ingredients in the Crock-Pot® slow cooker. Cover; cook on Low 6 to 8 hours (or on High for 3 to 4 hours). Spoon into sterilized jars and process according to standard canning methods.

For a 5, 6 or 7-quart Crock-Pot® slow cooker, double all ingredients.

CREAMY LEMON CHEESECAKE

This light and moist cheesecake has a fresh hint of lemon and is elegant enough to serve at a dinner party.

Crust:
1¼ cups graham cracker crumbs
½ tsp. lemon zest, grated
¼ cup butter or margarine, melted

Filling:
2–8 oz. packages cream cheese, softened
⅔ cup granulated sugar
1 Tbs. cornstarch
2 tsp. fresh lemon zest, grated
2 Tbs. fresh lemon juice
2 large eggs

Preheat the oven to 350°F. Grease and flour the inside of the stoneware or the Crock-Pot® Bread 'N Cake Bake Pan (available through Rival). Combine the crust ingredients and press into the bake pan. Bake, uncovered, in the oven for 5 to 7 minutes. Set aside.

In a large mixing bowl, cream the cream cheese with an electric mixer until smooth. Add the sugar, cornstarch, lemon zest and lemon juice, and then beat in the eggs one at a time, until fluffy. Pour over the baked crust in the Bread 'N Cake Bake Pan. With the lid on the bake pan, place in the slow cooker. Cover and cook on High 2½ to 3 hours. Remove the bake pan from the stoneware and allow to cool. Cover and refrigerate for 6 hours before unmolding. Makes 8 servings.

It's best to make two of these delicious cheesecakes separately rather than doubling the ingredients for the larger sizes of Crock-Pot® slow cookers.

ALL-AMERICAN CHEESECAKE

The red, white, and blue colors of this cheesecake make it the perfect dessert for your Fourth of July party or any other patriotic occasion.

Crust:
1¼ cups graham cracker crumbs
¼ cup butter or margarine, melted

Filling:
2–8 oz. packages cream cheese, softened
½ cup sugar
3 Tbs. flour
3 large eggs
½ cup strawberry preserves
½ pint fresh blueberries
½ pint fresh strawberries, sliced
mint sprigs for garnish

Preheat the oven to 350°F. Grease and flour the inside of the stoneware or the Crock-Pot® Bread 'N Cake Bake Pan. Combine the crust ingredients and press into the bake pan. Bake, uncovered, in the oven for 5 to 7 minutes. Set aside.

In a large mixing bowl, cream the cream cheese with an electric mixer until smooth. Add the sugar and flour, and then beat in the eggs one at a time, until fluffy. Fold in the strawberry preserves. Pour over the baked crust in the prepared bake pan. With the lid on the bake pan, place in the slow cooker. Cover the stoneware; cook on High 2½ to 3 hours. Remove the bake pan from the stoneware and allow to cool. Cover and refrigerate for 6 hours before unmolding. Top the cheesecake with fresh blueberries and strawberry slices. Garnish with sprigs of mint. Makes 8 servings.

It's best to make two of these delicious cheesecakes separately rather than doubling the ingredients for the larger sizes of Crock-Pot® slow cookers.

RAISIN, WALNUT & SPICE CARROT CAKE

This classic cake is chock full of carrots, raisins, walnuts and pineapple, with flavorful hints of cinnamon, cloves and vanilla. Cream cheese frosting adds the perfect touch!

Cake:
2 large eggs
1 cup granulated sugar
⅔ cup vegetable oil
1½ cups all-purpose flour
1 tsp. baking soda
½ tsp. salt
1 tsp. ground cinnamon
¼ tsp. ground cloves
¾ cup grated carrots
¼ cup walnuts, chopped
¼ cup raisins
1–14 oz. can crushed pineapple in syrup, drained
1 tsp. vanilla extract

Frosting:
8 oz. cream cheese, softened
1 tsp. vanilla extract
2½ cups confectioner's sugar
3 Tbs. walnuts, finely chopped

Lightly grease and flour the stoneware or the Crock-Pot® Bread 'N Cake Bake Pan (available through Rival). Set aside. In a large mixing bowl, beat together the eggs, sugar and oil with an electric mixer. In a separate bowl, combine the flour, soda, salt, cinnamon and cloves, and add to the egg mixture, beating well. Stir in the carrots, walnuts, raisins, pineapple and vanilla extract. Pour the mixture into the prepared bake pan. Cover the bake pan and place in the slow cooker. Cover; bake on High for 2½ to 4 hours. Remove the cake from the stoneware and allow to cool.

To prepare the frosting, beat the cream cheese and vanilla extract in a medium mixing bowl until creamy and slowly add in the confectioner's sugar. Frost the top of the cooled cake and sprinkle the frosting with the finely chopped walnuts. Makes 12 servings.

It's best to make two of these delicious cakes separately rather than doubling the ingredients for the larger sizes of Crock-Pot® slow cookers.

CHERRY POUND CAKE

Dessert couldn't be an easier than this! Serve this fruit-filled pound cake with vanilla ice cream for an added treat.

1-16 oz. package pound cake mix
2 eggs, well beaten
1-16 oz. can cherries and juice

For a 5, 6 or 7-quart Crock-Pot® slow cooker, you may double all ingredients.

Lightly grease the inside of the stoneware or the Crock-Pot® Bread 'N Cake Bake Pan (available through Rival). In a medium mixing bowl, blend together the pound cake mix and the eggs. Fold in the canned cherries and juice. Pour the contents into the prepared bake pan and place in the slow cooker. Cover; cook on High 2½ to 3 hours. The cake is done when a toothpick is inserted and cleanly removed from the center of the cake. Let cool before removing the cake from the bake pan. Makes 8 servings.

AMAZING PEACH BUTTER

6 cups unsweetened peaches, chunkily pureed
3 cups granulated sugar
1 cup apricot nectar
1 tsp. vanilla

So easy, yet superb!

Combine all ingredients in the Crock-Pot® slow cooker. Cover; cook on High for 4 hours. After 2 hours, remove the cover to allow the fruit and juice to cook down. Spoon into hot sterilized jars and process according to standard canning methods.

You may double all the ingredients when using a 5, 6 or 7-quart Crock-Pot® slow cooker.

BROWNIE BOTTOMS

This warm chocolate dessert is best served with whipped cream or ice cream.

½ cup brown sugar

¾ cup water

2 Tbs. cocoa powder

2½ cups packaged brownie mix

1–2¾ oz. package instant chocolate pudding mix

½ cup milk chocolate chip morsels

2 eggs

3 Tbs. butter or margarine, melted

½ cup water

For a 5, 6 or 7-quart Crock-Pot® slow cooker, you may double all ingredients.

Lightly grease the Crock-Pot® slow cooker with non-stick cooking spray. In a small saucepan, combine the brown sugar, ¾ cup water and cocoa powder and bring to a boil. In a small bowl, combine the remaining ingredients to form a batter. Spread the batter into the stoneware, and pour the boiling mixture over this batter. Cover; cook on High for 1½ hours. Turn off the heat and let stand for 30 minutes. Serve warm. Makes 6 servings.

APPLE-STREUSEL CAKE

1–16 oz. package pound cake mix
1–14 oz. can chunky apple pie filling
¼ cup brown sugar
1 Tbs. flour
¼ cup finely chopped walnuts
2 tsp. cinnamon

The aroma of fresh cake, apples and spices baking will bring your family to the table in a flash!

Prepare the pound cake according to package directions. Pour the batter into a well-greased and floured stoneware or the Crock-Pot® Bread 'N Cake Bake pan (available through Rival). In a medium bowl, combine the remaining ingredients and pour over the cake batter. Place the covered pan in the slow cooker. Cover; bake on High 3 to 4 hours. Serve warm or cold. Makes 10 servings.

For a 5, 6 or 7-quart Crock-Pot® slow cooker, you may double all ingredients.

INDEX

A

All-American Cheesecake, 206–7
All-American Meatloaf, 137
Almond Rice Pudding, Orange, 192–93
Amazing Peach Butter, 211
Any Day of the Week Beef Chili, 54–55
Apples
    Apple-Streusel Cake, 213
    Classic Baked Apples, 198
    Curried Apple Chicken, 77
    Homestyle Apple Brown Betty, 201
    Rustic Cranberry-Apple Butter, 202
    Smoked Sausage with Cabbage and Apples, 131
Apricots
    Apricot Mustard Chicken, 73
    Fruit Skewers with Apricot-Ginger Dipping Sauce,
        34–35
    Strawberry-Apricot Sauce, 203
Arizona Black Bean Dip, 23
Arroz con Pollo, 118–19
Artichokes
    Artichoke Cheese Dip, 17
    Fresh Vegetable Paella, 26
    Herbed Artichoke Chicken, 156–57
Asian Lettuce Wraps, 184–85
Asian Spiced Chicken Wings, 21
Asian Sweet and Sour Shrimp, 95
Asparagus
    Fresh Vegetable and Three-Cheese Frittata, 41
    Turkey Madeira Tetrazzini, 85

B

Bananas
    Banana Nut Bread, 199
    Candied Bananas Foster, 197
Bangkok Steak Salad, 108–9
Barbecued Chicken Pizza, 136
Barbecued Pulled Pork Sandwiches, 130
Basil and Cinnamon Syrup Nectarines, 191
BBQ Turkey Smokey Joes, 82
Beans, 12
    Any Day of the Week Beef Chili, 54–55
    Arizona Black Bean Dip, 23
    Bean and Corn Chili, 174–75
    Black Bean Stuffed Peppers, 176
    Classic Baked Beans, 145
    Easy Family-Style Tacos, 127
    Hearty Black Bean Soup, 113
    Kinpura Gobo, 120
    Milano Minestrone Soup, 107
    Moros, 121
    Savory Chicken Chili, 68
    Sloppy Dogs, 134
Beef
    Any Day of the Week Beef Chili, 54–55
    Bangkok Steak Salad, 108–9
    Beef and Button Mushroom Stroganoff, 50–51
    Cheese and Chile Enchilada Casserole, 104–5
    Chinese Hot Pot, 178–79
    Citrus Beef Stew, 172–73
    Classic Italian Beef Spaghetti, 129

Easy Barbecue Ribs, 135
Easy Family-Style Tacos, 127
French Beef Burgundy, 47
Grandmother's Stuffed Peppers, 57
Indonesian Beef Rendang, 101
Italian-Style Roast, 46
Kinpura Gobo, 120
Mango Spiced Ribs, 36
Niku Jaga, 114
Ropa Vieja, 122–23
Salsa Steak Fajitas, 112
Spinach and Feta-Stuffed Meatloaf, 48–49
Stuffed Cabbage Leaves, 144
Summertime Beef and Garden Vegetable
    Salad, 52–53
Sunday Dinner Beef Roast, 45
Tangerine Broccoli Beef, 56
Traditional Corned Beef and Cabbage, 58
Wild Mushroom Beef Stew, 44
Zesty Italian Barbecue Meatballs, 22
Bell peppers
    Black Bean Stuffed Peppers, 176
    Grandmother's Stuffed Peppers, 57
    Salsa Steak Fajitas, 112
    Tri-Pepper Southwestern Penne, 166
Black Bean Stuffed Peppers, 176
Blueberries
    All-American Cheesecake, 206–7
Braised Winter Squash, 170
Bread
    Banana Nut Bread, 199
    Chocolate Coffee Bread Pudding, 190

Coconut Bread Pudding, 188
    tips for, 13
Broccoli Beef, Tangerine, 56
Brown Betty, Homestyle Apple, 201
Brownie Bottoms, 212
Browning, 13
Brunch Florentine, 37
Burdock roots
    Kinpura Gobo, 120

C
Cabbage
    Bangkok Steak Salad, 108–9
    Smoked Sausage with Cabbage and Apples, 131
    Stuffed Cabbage Leaves, 144
    Traditional Corned Beef and Cabbage, 58
Cajun Chicken and Shrimp Creole, 154–55
Cakes
    Apple-Streusel Cake, 213
    Candied Bananas Foster, 197
    Cherry Pound Cake, 210
    Pumpkin Spice Cake, 200
    Raisin, Walnut and Spice Carrot Cake, 208–9
    tips for, 13
Candied Bananas Foster, 197
Caribbean Pork Chops, 60
Carrots
    Golden Roasted Root Vegetables, 30
    Parsnip and Carrot Soup, 148
    Raisin, Walnut and Spice Carrot Cake, 208–9
Cheese
    Artichoke Cheese Dip, 17

Cheese and Chile Enchilada Casserole, 104–5
Classic Cheese Fondue, 32
Corn and Cheese Chowder, 126
Fresh Vegetable and Three-Cheese Frittata, 41
Hearty Cheese Hash Browns, 38
Migas, 40
Mom's Best Macaroni and Cheese Dinner, 128
Salmon and Parmesan Rice Casserole, 94
Spinach and Feta-Stuffed Meatloaf, 48–49
Cheesecakes
   All-American Cheesecake, 206–7
   Creamy Lemon Cheesecake, 204–5
Cherry Pound Cake, 210
Chicken
   Apricot Mustard Chicken, 73
   Arroz con Pollo, 118–19
   Asian Lettuce Wraps, 184–85
   Asian Spiced Chicken Wings, 21
   Barbecued Chicken Pizza, 136
   Cajun Chicken and Shrimp Creole, 154–55
   Chicken and Fresh Vegetable Noodle Soup, 149
   Chicken and Sweet Potato Stew, 177
   Chicken and Vegetable Lasagne, 78–79
   Chicken Breasts with Wild Mushrooms, 152–53
   Chicken Chow Mein, 140–41
   Chicken Cordon Bleu Rolls, 75
   Chicken Pot au Feu, 168
   Chicken Provençal, 74
   Cool Chicken Curry Salad, 169
   Curried Apple Chicken, 77
   Green Tomatillo Chicken, 71
   Herbed Artichoke Chicken, 156–57

Herbed Garlic Chicken, 69
Homestyle Chicken and Dumplings, 138–39
Honey Hoisin Chicken, 72
Indonesian Coconut Chicken, 106
Islander Chicken Drumsticks, 132
Marinated Chinese Chicken Salad, 80–81
Pesto-Stuffed Chicken Breasts, 76
Roast Chicken with Peas, Prosciutto and Cream, 70
Savory Chicken Chili, 68
Shrimp Jambalaya, 92
Summer's Bounty Chicken and Fresh
   Vegetables, 162–63
Thai Green Curry, 116
Chile peppers
   Cheese and Chile Enchilada Casserole, 104–5
   cooking with, 60
   Green Chile Corn Dip, 18
Chili
   Any Day of the Week Beef Chili, 54–55
   Bean and Corn Chili, 174–75
   Savory Chicken Chili, 68
Chinese Hot Pot, 178–79
Chocolate
   Brownie Bottoms, 212
   Chocolate Coffee Bread Pudding, 190
Chowders
   Corn and Cheese Chowder, 126
   Creamy New England Clam Chowder, 93
Chow Mein, Chicken, 140–41
Cinnamon Ginger Poached Pears, 189
Cioppino, San Francisco, 91
Citrus Beef Stew, 172–73

Clams
    Clams Florentine, 97
    Creamy New England Clam Chowder, 93
Classic Baked Apples, 198
Classic Baked Beans, 145
Classic Cheese Fondue, 32
Classic Italian Beef Spaghetti, 129
Cobbler, Peach, with Lavender Syrup, 194–95
Coconut and coconut milk
    Candied Bananas Foster, 197
    Coconut Bread Pudding, 188
    Indonesian Beef Rendang, 101
    Indonesian Coconut Chicken, 106
    Thai Green Curry, 116
Cool Chicken Curry Salad, 169
Corn
    Bean and Corn Chili, 174–75
    Corn and Cheese Chowder, 126
    Green Chile Corn Dip, 18
    Turkey Tamale Pie, 86
Corned Beef and Cabbage, Traditional, 58
Country Scalloped Potatoes with Ham, 24
Cozumel Tortilla Soup, 100
Crab
    Crab and Spinach Lasagne, 164
    Hot Crab Dip, 20
Cranberries
    Cranberry-Mustard Pork Tenderloin, 62
    Cranberry-Orange Turkey Breast, 84
    Rustic Cranberry-Apple Butter, 202
Creamy Curried Spinach, 25
Creamy Lemon Cheesecake, 204–5

Creamy New England Clam Chowder, 93
Creamy Spinach Dip, 19
Cucumber Raita, 111
Curries
    Cool Chicken Curry Salad, 169
    Curried Apple Chicken, 77
    Thai Green Curry, 116

D
Desserts
    All-American Cheesecake, 206–7
    Apple-Streusel Cake, 213
    Banana Nut Bread, 199
    Basil and Cinnamon Syrup Nectarines, 191
    Brownie Bottoms, 212
    Candied Bananas Foster, 197
    Cherry Pound Cake, 210
    Chocolate Coffee Bread Pudding, 190
    Cinnamon Ginger Poached Pears, 189
    Classic Baked Apples, 198
    Coconut Bread Pudding, 188
    Creamy Lemon Cheesecake, 204–5
    Homestyle Apple Brown Betty, 201
    Orange Almond Rice Pudding, 192–93
    Peach Cobbler with Lavender Syrup, 194–95
    Pumpkin Spice Cake, 200
    Raisin, Walnut and Spice Carrot Cake, 208–9
    Strawberry and Rhubarb Pandowdy, 196
Dips
    Arizona Black Bean Dip, 23
    Artichoke Cheese Dip, 17
    Creamy Spinach Dip, 19

Green Chile Corn Dip, 18
Hot Crab Dip, 20
Dumplings, Homestyle Chicken and, 138–39

E

Easy Barbecue Ribs, 135
Easy Family-Style Tacos, 127
Easy Italian Sausage Scramble, 39
Eggs
    Brunch Florentine, 37
    Fresh Vegetable and Three-Cheese Frittata, 41
    Migas, 40

F

Fajitas, Salsa Steak, 112
Fish. *See also* Seafood, mixed
    Halibut Steaks in a Lemony Wine Sauce, 96
    Halibut with Tomato Tapenade, 158
    Salmon and Parmesan Rice Casserole, 94
Fondue, Classic Cheese, 32
French Beef Burgundy, 47
French Onion Soup, 115
Fresh Herbed Turkey Breast, 87
Fresh Vegetable and Three-Cheese Frittata, 41
Fresh Vegetable Paella, 26–27
Frittata, Fresh Vegetable and Three-Cheese, 41
Frozen foods, 12
Fruit Skewers with Apricot-Ginger Dipping Sauce, 34–35

G

Golden Roasted Root Vegetables, 30

Grandmother's Stuffed Peppers, 57
Green Chile Corn Dip, 18
Green Tomatillo Chicken, 71

H

Halibut
    Halibut Steaks in a Lemony Wine Sauce, 96
    Halibut with Tomato Tapenade, 158
Ham
    Country Scalloped Potatoes with Ham, 24
    Shrimp Jambalaya, 92
Hash Browns, Hearty Cheese, 38
Hearty Black Bean Soup, 113
Hearty Cheese Hash Browns, 38
Herbed Artichoke Chicken, 156–57
Herbed Garlic Chicken, 69
Herbs, 13
Herb-Sprinkled Scalloped Potatoes, 160–61
Homestyle Apple Brown Betty, 201
Homestyle Chicken and Dumplings, 138–39
Honey Hoisin Chicken, 72
Hop Sing Sweet and Sour Pork, 142–43
Hot Crab Dip, 20
Hot dogs
    Sloppy Dogs, 134

I

Ice cream
    Candied Bananas Foster, 197
    toppings for, 202, 203
Indian Lamb Korma, 110
Indonesian Beef Rendang, 101

Indonesian Coconut Chicken, 106
Islander Chicken Drumsticks, 132
Italian-Style Roast, 46

J
Jambalaya, Shrimp, 92

K
Kinpura Gobo, 120

L
Lamb
    Indian Lamb Korma, 110
    Lamb Chops with Red Wine Glaze, 65
    Lamb Shank Tangine, 63
    Lamb with Balsamic-Glazed Vegetables, 171
    Stuffed Lamb Roast, 64
Lasagne
    Chicken and Vegetable Lasagne, 78–79
    Crab and Spinach Lasagne, 164
Lavender Syrup, Peach Cobbler with, 194–95
Lemons
    Creamy Lemon Cheesecake, 204–5
    Lemon-Garlic Turkey Breast, 88
Lentil Soup, Spiced, 150–51
Lettuce Wraps, Asian, 184–85

M
Macaroni and Cheese Dinner, Mom's Best, 128
Mango Spiced Ribs, 36
Marinated Chinese Chicken Salad, 80–81
Marmalade, Red Onion, 33

Meatballs, Zesty Italian Barbecue, 22
Meatloaf
    All-American Meatloaf, 137
    Spinach and Feta-Stuffed Meatloaf, 48–49
Mediterranean Turkey and Tomato Rice Bake, 159
Migas, 40
Milano Minestrone Soup, 107
Milk, adding, 11
Minestrone Soup, Milano, 107
Mom's Best Macaroni and Cheese Dinner, 128
Moros, 121
Mushrooms
    Beef and Button Mushroom Stroganoff, 50–51
    Brunch Florentine, 37
    Chicken Breasts with Wild Mushrooms, 152–53
    Wild Mushroom Beef Stew, 44

N
Nectarines, Basil and Cinnamon Syrup, 191
Niku Jaga, 114
Noodles. See Pasta and noodles

O
Onions
    French Onion Soup, 115
    Red Onion Marmalade, 33
Orange Almond Rice Pudding, 192–93

P
Paella
    Fresh Vegetable Paella, 26–27
    Valencian Seafood Paella, 90

Pandowdy, Strawberry and Rhubarb, 196
Parsnips
    Golden Roasted Root Vegetables, 30
    Parsnip and Carrot Soup, 148
Pasta and noodles, 11
    Beef and Button Mushroom Stroganoff, 50–51
    Chicken and Fresh Vegetable Noodle Soup, 149
    Chicken and Vegetable Lasagne, 78–79
    Chicken Breasts with Wild Mushrooms, 152–53
    Chicken Chow Mein, 140–41
    Clams Florentine, 97
    Classic Italian Beef Spaghetti, 129
    Crab and Spinach Lasagne, 164
    Marinated Chinese Chicken Salad, 80–81
    Milano Minestrone Soup, 107
    Mom's Best Macaroni and Cheese Dinner, 128
    Parsnip and Carrot Soup, 148
    Pizza Pasta, 133
    Tarragon Turkey and Pasta, 83
    Tomato and Basil Ziti with Roasted
        Vegetables, 182–83
    Tri-Pepper Southwestern Penne, 166
    Turkey Madeira Tetrazzini, 85
Peaches
    Amazing Peach Butter, 211
    Peach Cobbler with Lavender Syrup, 194–95
Pears, Cinnamon Ginger Poached, 189
Peas
    Fresh Vegetable Paella, 26–27
    Roast Chicken with Peas, Prosciutto and Cream, 70
    Valencian Seafood Paella, 90
Pesto-Stuffed Chicken Breasts, 76

Pineapple
    Asian Sweet and Sour Shrimp, 95
    Fruit Skewers with Apricot-Ginger Dipping Sauce,
        34–35
    Hop Sing Sweet and Sour Pork, 142–43
    Islander Chicken Drumsticks, 132
    Polynesian Pork Roast, 61
    Raisin, Walnut and Spice Carrot Cake, 208–9
    Summer's Bounty Chicken and Fresh
        Vegetables, 162–63
Pizza, Barbecued Chicken, 136
Pizza Pasta, 133
Polynesian Pork Roast, 61
Pork
    Barbecued Pulled Pork Sandwiches, 130
    Caribbean Pork Chops, 60
    Cranberry-Mustard Pork Tenderloin, 62
    Easy Barbecue Ribs, 135
    Hop Sing Sweet and Sour Pork, 142–43
    Polynesian Pork Roast, 61
    Pork Loin with Sherry and Red Onions, 59
Potatoes
    Country Scalloped Potatoes with Ham, 24
    Creamy New England Clam Chowder, 93
    Easy Italian Sausage Scramble, 39
    Golden Roasted Root Vegetables, 30
    Hearty Cheese Hash Browns, 38
    Herb-Sprinkled Scalloped Potatoes, 160–61
    Rosemary Red Jacket Potatoes, 31
    Vichyssoise, 117
Prosciutto
    Chicken Cordon Bleu Rolls, 75

Roast Chicken with Peas, Prosciutto and Cream, 70
Puddings
    Chocolate Coffee Bread Pudding, 190
    Coconut Bread Pudding, 188
    Orange Almond Rice Pudding, 192–93
Pumpkin Spice Cake, 200

R
Raisin, Walnut and Spice Carrot Cake, 208–9
Raita, Cucumber, 111
Ratatouille, Summer Vegetable, 28–29
Red Onion Marmalade, 33
Rhubarb and Strawberry Pandowdy, 196
Ribs
    Easy Barbecue Ribs, 135
    Mango Spiced Ribs, 36
Rice, 11
    Arroz con Pollo, 118–19
    Cajun Chicken and Shrimp Creole, 154–55
    Fresh Vegetable Paella, 26–27
    Grandmother's Stuffed Peppers, 57
    Honey Hoisin Chicken, 72
    Mediterranean Turkey and Tomato Rice Bake, 159
    Moros, 121
    Orange Almond Rice Pudding, 192–93
    Salmon and Parmesan Rice Casserole, 94
    Shrimp Jambalaya, 92
    Stuffed Cabbage Leaves, 144
    Tangerine Broccoli Beef, 56
    Valencian Seafood Paella, 90
Roast Chicken with Peas, Prosciutto and Cream, 70
Ropa Vieja, 122–23

Rosemary Red Jacket Potatoes, 31
Rustic Cranberry-Apple Butter, 202

S
Safety, 12
Salads
    Bangkok Steak Salad, 108–9
    Cool Chicken Curry Salad, 169
    Marinated Chinese Chicken Salad, 80–81
    Summertime Beef and Garden Vegetable Salad, 52–53
Salmon and Parmesan Rice Casserole, 94
Salsa Steak Fajitas, 112
Sandwiches
    Barbecued Pulled Pork Sandwiches, 130
    BBQ Turkey Smokey Joes, 82
    Sloppy Dogs, 134
San Francisco Cioppino, 91
Sausage
    Easy Italian Sausage Scramble, 39
    Shrimp Jambalaya, 92
    Smoked Sausage with Cabbage and Apples, 131
Savory Chicken Chili, 68
Seafood, mixed. *See also individual types of seafood*
    San Francisco Cioppino, 91
    Southeast Asian Seafood Stew, 102–3
    Valencian Seafood Paella, 90
Shrimp
    Asian Sweet and Sour Shrimp, 95
    Cajun Chicken and Shrimp Creole, 154–55
    Shrimp Jambalaya, 92
Sloppy Dogs, 134

Smoked Sausage with Cabbage and Apples, 131
Soups. *See also* Chowders
    Chicken and Fresh Vegetable Noodle Soup, 149
    Chinese Hot Pot, 178–79
    Cozumel Tortilla Soup, 100
    French Onion Soup, 115
    Hearty Black Bean Soup, 113
    Milano Minestrone Soup, 107
    Parsnip and Carrot Soup, 148
    Spiced Lentil Soup, 150–51
    Vichyssoise, 117
Sour cream, adding, 11
Southeast Asian Seafood Stew, 102–3
Spiced Lentil Soup, 150–51
Spices, 13
Spinach
    Brunch Florentine, 37
    Clams Florentine, 97
    Crab and Spinach Lasagne, 164
    Creamy Curried Spinach, 25
    Creamy Spinach Dip, 19
    Spinach and Feta-Stuffed Meatloaf, 48–49
Squash
    Braised Winter Squash, 170
    Fresh Vegetable and Three-Cheese Frittata, 41
    Summer's Bounty Chicken and Fresh
        Vegetables, 162–63
    Summer Vegetable Ratatouille, 28–29
Stirring, 11
Stoneware, Removable, 12–13
Strawberries
    All-American Cheesecake, 206–7
    Fruit Skewers with Apricot-Ginger Dipping
        Sauce, 34–35
    Strawberry and Rhubarb Pandowdy, 196
    Strawberry-Apricot Sauce, 203
Stuffed Cabbage Leaves, 144
Stuffed Lamb Roast, 64
Summer's Bounty Chicken and Fresh Vegetables, 162–63
Summertime Beef and Garden Vegetable Salad, 52–53
Summer Vegetable Ratatouille, 28–29
Sunday Dinner Beef Roast, 45
Sweet Potato and Chicken Stew, 177

T
Tacos, Easy Family-Style, 127
Tangerine Broccoli Beef, 56
Tangine, Lamb Shank, 63
Tarragon Turkey and Pasta, 83
Temperatures, 12
Thai Green Curry, 116
Tips, 11–13
Tomatillo Chicken, Green, 71
Tomatoes
    Any Day of the Week Beef Chili, 54–55
    Arroz con Pollo, 118–19
    Chicken and Sweet Potato Stew, 177
    Chicken Provençal, 74
    Classic Italian Beef Spaghetti, 129
    Cozumel Tortilla Soup, 100
    Halibut with Tomato Tapenade, 158
    Italian-Style Roast, 46
    Mediterranean Turkey and Tomato Rice Bake, 159
    Milano Minestrone Soup, 107

Pizza Pasta, 133
San Francisco Cioppino, 91
Shrimp Jambalaya, 92
Spiced Lentil Soup, 150–51
Tomato and Basil Ziti with Roasted
     Vegetables, 182–83
Tri-Pepper Southwestern Penne, 166
Turkey Tamale Pie, 86
Tortilla chips
     Cozumel Tortilla Soup, 100
     Migas, 40
Traditional Corned Beef and Cabbage, 58
Tri-Pepper Southwestern Penne, 166
Turkey
     All-American Meatloaf, 137
     Asian Lettuce Wraps, 184–85
     BBQ Turkey Smokey Joes, 82
     Cranberry-Orange Turkey Breast, 84
     Fresh Herbed Turkey Breast, 87
     Lemon-Garlic Turkey Breast, 88
     Mediterranean Turkey and Tomato Rice Bake, 159
     Tarragon Turkey and Pasta, 83
     Turkey Madeira Tetrazzini, 85
     Turkey Tamale Pie, 86
Tuscan Vegetable Torte, 180–81

V
Valencian Seafood Paella, 90
Vegetables. *See also individual vegetables*
     Chicken and Fresh Vegetable Noodle Soup, 149
     Chicken and Vegetable Lasagne, 78–79
     Chicken Pot au Feu, 168

Chinese Hot Pot, 178–79
Citrus Beef Stew, 172–73
Fresh Vegetable and Three-Cheese Frittata, 41
Fresh Vegetable Paella, 26–27
Golden Roasted Root Vegetables, 30
Lamb with Balsamic-Glazed Vegetables, 171
Milano Minestrone Soup, 107
Summer's Bounty Chicken and Fresh
     Vegetables, 162–63
Summertime Beef and Garden Vegetable Salad, 52–53
Summer Vegetable Ratatouille, 28–29
Tomato and Basil Ziti with Roasted
     Vegetables, 182–83
Tri-Pepper Southwestern Penne, 166
Tuscan Vegetable Torte, 180–81
Vichyssoise, 117

W
Walnuts
     Banana Nut Bread, 199
     Raisin, Walnut and Spice Carrot Cake, 208–9
Wild Mushroom Beef Stew, 44
Wine, cooking with, 65

Z
Zesty Italian Barbecue Meatballs, 22
Ziti, Tomato and Basil, with Roasted Vegetables, 182–83
Zucchini
     Fresh Vegetable and Three-Cheese Frittata, 41
     Summer's Bounty Chicken and Fresh
          Vegetables, 162–63
     Summer Vegetable Ratatouille, 28–29